STALKING THE SHARK

Pressure and Passion on the Pro Golf Tour

STALKING
THE
SHARK

Pressure and Passion on the Pro Golf Tour

CARL VIGELAND

W. W. NORTON & COMPANY

NEW YORK / LONDON

For information about permission to reproduce selections from this book,
write to Permissions, W. W. Norton & Company, Inc.,
500 Fifth Avenue, New York, NY 10110.

The text of this book is composed in Palatino with the display set in Radiant
Composition and Manufacturing by the Haddon Craftsmen, Inc.
Book design by Jam Design

Library of Congress Cataloging-in-Publication Data

Vigeland, Carl A.
    Stalking the shark : pressure and passion on the pro golf tour /
Carl Vigeland.
        p.   cm.
    ISBN 0-393-03795-9
    1. Golf—Tournaments.   2. Professional Golfer's Association of
America.   3. Norman, Greg, 1955–   .
I. Title.
GV970.V55   1996
796.352´66—dc20
    [B]   95-25470

W. W. Norton & Company, Inc., 500 Fifth Avenue, New York, N.Y. 10110
                    http://web.wwnorton.com
W. W. Norton & Company Ltd., 10 Coptic Street, London WC1A 1PU

1 2 3 4 5 6 7 8 9 0

For my son,
Christian

Experience is a wonderful thing.
　　　　　　　　　—GREG NORMAN

CONTENTS

Photographs appear following page 128.

STALKING THE SHARK

Pressure and Passion on the Pro Golf Tour

OCTOBER 31, 1993

THE BUZZ IN the air from the disbelieving crowd was still rising audibly, a collective nervous chatter straining to comprehend what had happened—*again!*—when the two principals
had a remarkable exchange.

"Sorry about that, Greg," said the victor, Jim Gallagher, Jr.,
before continuing with an interview on national television.

Greg Norman's head nodded in acknowledgment, but his
ashen expression remained unchanged.

Minutes before, even spectators watching from the cozy
comfort of the tent next to the television booth reflexively dried
the palms of their hands. Would the man everyone could see
in the distance pondering his club selection hit the right shot?

Greg Norman knew that if you stand near the back of the
eighteenth green at the Olympic Club and drop a golf ball, it
will almost immediately begin to roll away from you, toward
the front. He knew, therefore, that he must keep his approach
shot on this short, uphill par four below the hole. That way he
would have an uphill putt. With an uphill putt he could try to
make birdie or leave himself with something short for his par.
But with a downhill putt, especially one on greens as fast as
Olympic's, he might not only miss the hole with his putt but

watch in horror as his ball picked up speed and ran right off the green.

Despite the greenside bunkers in front, keeping the ball below the hole did not present a severe physical problem to a golfer of such extraordinary skill as Greg Norman, an athlete so good and so famous that he had two names by which he was known, without the use of his last name. Not just the anxious fans at the Olympic Club that day but people in and around golf everywhere in the world had only to say Greg and it was apparent whom they meant. Or they could call him by his nickname. The Shark.

He was the golfer all the other players talked about, even when he wasn't around—especially when he wasn't around. There was a part of Greg Norman in each one of them, though few would admit it. Even when they criticized him, which they did frequently, the basis of their criticism, the foundation from which it stemmed, was awe. Awe mixed with envy and pettiness and begrudging respect.

"He's only won two majors," someone who had won none would observe. "What's he got, twelve victories in the States? Lots of good players have more than that." Such remarks were usually made with passion, though they often lacked authority. That was part of the complication of Greg's place in golf, but by no means the whole explanation, another part of which lay in the bizarre litany of near-wins Norman had achieved over the years: the 1986 bunker shot by Bob Tway that cost him that year's PGA Championship (or was it really the poor play earlier in the round?), the Masters playoff chip-in by Larry Mize that left Greg tied for second at Augusta in 1987 . . . the list was long, well known, and somehow still mysterious or perhaps irrelevant (hadn't Jack Nicklaus, the all-time leader in so-called majors, also finished *second* in majors more than anyone else?).

Notwithstanding the debate these questions inspired, Norman somehow combined in all the attributes he brought to the game the ideal of a golfer, while his occasional misuse of the tremendous skills at his disposal—such touch! such distance!—betrayed the very real, very human athlete usually hidden inside the protective armor of his famous persona. A man known to millions of people around the world who in a moment of reflection could maintain he had very few friends in his adopted country, an enigma whose failures and victories alike were the stuff of dreams.

The day before, playing with Jay Haas in the third round, the Shark had finished with a flourish. After a birdie at seventeen, he hit a fine drive on eighteen.

"One hundred and eight," his caddy, Tony Navaro, told him, meaning the number of yards to the pin.

Greg hit a pitching wedge, and the ball stopped two feet from the pin.

Now that man focused on his shot, probably a nine-iron to keep the ball below the hole.

Inexplicably, he chose an eight.

"A mental mistake."

That is what he called it later, after the eight-iron of course went long and he had an impossible downhill chip so that he had to aim for the fringe, where the ball hopped onto the green and shot past the hole, leaving him a par putt that he missed, a par putt that would have forced a playoff with Jim Gallagher. Though Gallagher had shot a course-record 63 the first day of the four-day tournament, he was stunned to realize he had defeated Norman for the championship. At that point in his ten-year professional career, Gallagher had won a total of two tournaments. Now he had just beaten the world's best for a first prize that was almost as much money as he had ever earned in an entire season.

By the time the Shark had signed his scorecard after putting out on the eighteenth, Gallagher had commenced with his interview. Norman had to pass him as he walked up an embankment toward the clubhouse, and Gallagher paused to acknowledge him. "Sorry about that, Greg."

SHARKBITE

EARLY ON I asked myself what I wanted out of the game of golf. And I said to myself, "I want to be a professional golfer." Then I said to myself, "If you want to be a professional golfer, what commitment are you going to give?" Well, that commitment is to be the best I can be at the game of golf. "To be the best you can be at the game of golf, what do you have to do to get there?" Give a lot of dedication, a lot of sacrifice.

I mean that. Sacrifice.

When I was a kid growing up, I didn't go out partying and have a great time.

When I was twenty-one, I hit the road.

And I did it on my own. There was no guarantee of my success. I didn't have any sponsor, I just hit the road myself.

I made the sacrifices you have to make. Then they started to pay off. Then I started to feel confident that I had made the right decision, that I'd paved the right road, I'm going down the main stream that I want to go down.

But you're never going to get *there*.

The day you think you've climbed the mountain, there's only one way to go. If you think you've reached the top, there's one way to go, and that's down to the bottom. When you start sliding down the other side of that mountain, you can dig your fingernails and toenails into the side of the mountain and try to stop yourself from sliding and slow down, but it is almost impossible to stop yourself and start climbing back up again.

And I've experienced that. I can tell you from both sides of the spectrum on this deal, when I was at the top of the world I went flying down to the bottom of the world. It was my fault, it was self-imposed. I could see that what I was doing was wrong. And I stuck my fingernails into the ground to stop myself. And then I said, "Boy, you are back to ground zero, where you were, and you've got to go back and do the same things again."

So I did.

SAN FRANCISCO

A YEAR HAD passed. It was the last afternoon of the last tournament of another professional golf season.

A few hours earlier, Mark McCumber, a mid-career pro with a quirky swing and a habit of chatting with the gallery between shots, had won the tournament's $540,000 first prize. Now, while McCumber and his family and friends were celebrating at a Fisherman's Wharf restaurant, the men and a few women who earned their living writing and talking about Mark McCumber and the other golfers on the PGA Tour were still laboring in the pressroom of the Olympic Club—a posh private playground in the southwestern corner of San Francisco, overlooking the Pacific Ocean—because their planned stories about third-round leader Bill Glasson or such colorful pursuers as the young U.S. Open winner Ernie Els had to be scrapped in favor of features about the perfectly talented but rather plain McCumber, a devoutly religious man so relentlessly upbeat that he even cheered on his opponents.

Clocks on the wall told the time in Tokyo and Australia. One of the supremely organized people from the tour who had run the tournament had arranged for box lunches to be left in the dining alcove just off the pressroom. Unwatched, a professional football game from the East Coast played on the television there, near a table stacked high with many copies of the Bay Area Sunday newspapers. In most of those newspapers, filled with stories about the war in Bosnia-Herzegovina and the upcoming Congressional elections, the sports section was missing, having been taken earlier in the day by one of the many media personnel, as they were officially referred to, who had been covering this tournament. The rest of the sections in most of those newspapers had been untouched.

Behind the left, middle section of press tables, network radio announcers were still taping reports about McCumber and the amazing number—four!—of near-wins second-place finisher Fuzzy Zoeller had had this season. Had anyone else ever come so close so often?

"Hey, what was it that Fuzzy said he was drinking afterward?" a voice from another section of the room called out. The question referred to the size of the vodka and tonic the famously easygoing Zoeller had enjoyed during his post-tournament press conference.

"A triple!" came the immediate answer.

This had been the second of two annual Tour Championships played on the Olympic Club's Lake Course. The year before, in an excruciatingly painful performance, golf's Great White Shark, Greg Norman, had bogeyed four of the last seven holes to lose not only the tournament but that season's title as top money winner and, probably by virtue of the loss, the vote of his peers as player of the year.

IN THE INTERVIEW room after the second day of that 1993 Tour Championship, the Shark recited details of his round.

"On number one, I hit driver and four iron. On number four, three-wood and eight-iron. Number nine, driver and eight-iron. Number eleven, driver and seven-iron. Number thirteen, a five-iron."

The players all had the ability to remember what they did in this way, many of them seemingly able to recall shot by shot details of rounds they played years ago.

In response to a question about Nick Price, his playing partner that day, Greg said, "Nick played pretty good; not crisp."

Afterward, he greeted his wife, Laura, outside the room.

"Hi, honey," he said, and they kissed.

HIS INITIALS DECORATE the wings of his plane. He calls his home in Hobe Sound "Tranquility." His latest (ninety-foot) designer "fishing boat" is the *Aussie Rules,* a one-of-a-kind extravagance for which he paid a reported $6 million.

The dog's name is Foster, after the beer. His favorite Australian beer is VB.

The first two golf books he read were by Jack Nicklaus, *Golf My Way* and *55 Ways to Play Golf.*

His first golf job was as apprentice pro at Royal Queensland Golf Club, where he earned $28 a week in 1976.

He first played in the United States in Nicklaus's tournament, the Memorial, which he would win twice in the 1990s. But he missed the cut in 1977.

He led the European tour in money in 1982.

He lost to journeyman Mike Nicolette in a playoff in the Bay Hill Classic in 1983, his first tournament during his first full year on the PGA Tour.

In 1986, the year he won his first British Open, he claims he was broke.

He began working with teacher Butch Harmon in 1991, the *only* year since turning pro that he did not win a professional golf tournament somewhere in the world.

Under Harmon, his swing became slightly flatter and decidedly shorter. Harmon also worked with Greg on upper and lower body rotation.

Golf ratings on CBS are significantly higher when Norman is in contention.

He invested $2 million in the golf equipment company Cobra for a 12 percent share of the company. That share was worth an estimated $84 million in 1995.

GUARDED BY A huge man from Athens, Georgia, named Tiny, a beautiful buffet of food was served for the players in the Olympic Club locker room. But the players spent very little time there enjoying their sumptuous feast. They were either warming up, playing, or practicing, or they were eating upstairs in the very fancy dining room with their wives.

This fact did not keep Tiny, a Pinkerton employee who was present at many tournaments, from doing his job. Nonplayers were not allowed to snack. And anyone without the proper credential to be in the room was politely but very firmly told to leave. There were no exceptions. At a U.S. Open where he was guarding the entrance to the media tent, Tiny refused entrance to a writer he knew because the man had the wrong badge. Tiny called the man "sir." A woman might be addressed as "honey."

IN 1994 THE stakes had changed for Norman, whose statistical ranking as the world's number one professional golfer had been overtaken by his friend Nick Price, a Zimbabwean who since 1991 had been on a tear, winning tournaments at a faster clip than anyone in more than a decade.

And a year later the golf world was buzzing over the emergence of the precocious, powerful Ernie Els from South Africa, whose Open win had come in June. In San Francisco at the end of October, where the top thirty money winners of the year were competing, Els was the golfing subject of numerous repeated conversations among the golf experts hanging out on the range and around the practice greens of the Olympic Club.

Friday

"WHAT DO YOU think of Els's swing?" Jaime Diaz pensively asked Billy Harmon late on the Friday afternoon of tournament week. Els that day had shot 67, good for a second-place tie, and now he was practicing his putts. Diaz, an articulate former college golfer who grew up in the Bay Area, resigned his position as chief golf scribe for the *New York Times* to write for *Sports Illustrated*'s special golf section, included weekly in an edition of the magazine targeted for subscribers who had been identified as golfers. Dressed out of uniform in blue jeans, the diminutive Harmon, one of the sons of former Masters champion Claude Harmon, Sr., is the teaching pro at the Newport (Rhode Island) Country Club; his brother is Greg Norman's coach, Butch.

Harmon's response to Diaz's question that day was immediate and direct.

"Els's swing is one not marred by fear or thought," Harmon observed.

This observation was soon followed by comments about the reason for everyone being where they were. Golf, Billy Harmon quoted another, past golf observer, George Knudsen, is a game "in which you give up control to gain control." To hear such words in the setting of the Olympic Club's upper putting green was akin to being in church and listening to a cleric intone a familiar Biblical passage. Words that, in another context, might sound clichéd could suddenly assume a fresh significance. Perhaps Billy Harmon understood something about golf that explained its completely absorbing hold on the people who, like Diaz and Harmon himself, organized their lives around it.

"Let me tell you something," Billy continued. "Now, I'm not going to mention the name of this one person, because I don't want to be picking on him, but he was hitting balls one day on the range and everyone said what a beautiful swing he had. And my father was there, but he was watching someone else.

He was watching Lee Trevino. Nothing classic about Lee Trevino's swing. But Lee was doing all these things with his golf swing, drawing the ball to spots on the range he picked out before each shot. And that's who my father was watching.

" 'Why are you watching Trevino?' someone asked my father.

" 'Because he has the best swing here,' my father replied.

" 'How can you say that?'

" 'Look where his ball ends up. The ball tells you who has the best swing.' "

If Billy Harmon's father had been here that day at the Olympic Club, another golfer he would have been watching was unheralded, often hurt, laconic Bill Glasson. Glasson's surprising scores for the first two days of the tournament were 66-68, giving him a total of 134, one stroke ahead of Ernie Els.

"Tell us about your round today."

That was the first question Bill Glasson had been asked at a press conference he had just held inside the magnificent clubhouse. And Glasson had dutifully obliged, in a ritual that was a staple at these sessions.

"I got off to a great start again, just like yesterday," Glasson said. "Good save on the fourth hole, and I birdied one again; hit it on in two to the left fringe and two-putted. I just kind of made some solid pars until seven. Hit a driver on seven just short of the green, and got it up and down for birdie. I made about a six-footer for birdie. And then on eight I hit an eight-iron about fifteen feet left of the hole and made that. And parred nine. Turned at three under [for the front nine]. That got me to eight under [for the tournament]."

In a deadpan monotone, Glasson continued with a description of the rest of his round before answering questions about his many knee operations and his favorite hobby, flying. Even seated, the usually laconic Glasson looked physically uncomfortable, as if just the exertion of shifting his body weight from the left to the right caused some slight pain. There was also something slightly subversive about his appearance; the deepest eyes and the long light-blond hair made him seem more like a drummer in a band of deadheads than an athlete on the most clean-cut, upbeat of tours.

"What is more fun for you, Billy," a reporter asked, "flying a plane or playing golf?" Though he prefers the name Bill, Glasson is usually called Billy within golfing circles, in keeping with a mysterious but nearly universal practice on tour, a country southernness of professional golf that is duplicated in much of football. Thus Nick Price is invariably called Nicky. There are exceptions to this nomenclature, particularly for golfers whose first names already end in y. (Announcing on television a putt by Duffy Waldorf, for example, Gary McCord says, "This looks like about a three-footer for the Duffmeister.")

"Stupid question," answered Billy, his tone unchanged. "I play golf so I can fly. I have to support my habit somehow."

Then he compared the two activities, calling them "a good combination.

"I mean, obviously golf is not life-threatening. Well, I guess it could be, in pro-ams. But the two overlap a lot. Golf is a game of precision, and you are always trying to do things perfectly. Flying is kind of the same way. You are always trying to shoot the perfect round, the perfect landing."

Saturday

THE NEXT DAY, after shooting another round that anyone but a professional would probably term perfect, Glasson was in even better form during the post-round Q&A. How did he feel about the prospect of being paired on Sunday with Fuzzy Zoeller, a golfer so loquacious and apparently loose that he whistled after a bad shot and chatted constantly with the gallery?

That would be no problem, Glasson replied; he and Fuzzy got along just fine.

"Except there's one thing that puzzles me."

What's that, Billy?

"Whenever I play with Fuzzy, he always calls me Dick."

There was a nervous twitter from somewhere in the rear of the room. Otherwise, silence.

"I don't know," Glasson continued. "Maybe he thinks my first name is Richard."

This remark, delivered in the same deadpan that characterized all of Glasson's repartee, was greeted with a few chuckles.

"Does he say 'Dick'? Or 'You dick'?" inquired an audience pundit. More laughter now.

"Just Dick."

Lots of laughter.

The next question concerned the other competitors Glasson thought might beat him.

"Greg Norman has a chance," Glasson said. "I know you guys give him a hard time for not winning more often over here, but how many other people, every time they tee it up, are in contention?"

This was apparently a rhetorical question, because Glasson did not wait for a response. Instead, he went on to claim that Greg Norman was arguably the finest golfer of his generation.

Gasp.

"What about Nick Faldo?" a defender of the former British Open champion asserted more than asked. Faldo, who had been supplanted in the world rankings by both Norman and Nick Price, was still a notorious curmudgeon on the golf course, well known for saying little if anything to his fellow competitors of the day other than, perhaps, "You're away."

Glasson stared straight ahead, never betraying a hint of interest in this forum. He might have been impersonating David Letterman.

"Now that's someone I call Dick," Glasson said, and the room erupted in prolonged laughter. Everyone but Glasson smiled.

Outside, as the repartee continued, the Shark practiced on the range before hitching a ride in a golf cart to inspect a new par-three course the club had built on the ocean side of State Highway 1. He appeared a little uncomfortable as he hopped on, as if his lean, muscular frame were not accustomed to such a lowly form of transport. He waved lamely to the fans who had been watching him—everywhere Norman goes on a golf course there are fans watching him—but a club official, dressed in spiffy slacks and a natty blazer, prohibited anyone else from coming along on that little excursion. The gate leading to the par three was locked after Norman's cart passed through, to keep out any stray members of the golfing public, people whose money tournaments welcome but whose presence clubs only tolerate. The social pecking order that at its zenith prohibits prospective club members from submitting applications to certain clubs—one doesn't *apply* to become a member of Pebble Beach's neighbor, Cypress Point, but is, in rarefied circumstances, *asked*—that hierarchy of status is reinforced at golf tournaments in subtle ways, such as the special badges that club members receive admitting them to viewing areas closed to mere ticket holders.

The golfers themselves seem largely unmoved by the exclusionary fuss that is made around them. Not many generations ago, men of their ilk were considered by the members of prominent clubs to be of an inferior social class. Now they are celebrities, fleetingly famous but, from the perspective of old money, embarrassingly in need of working for a living. A club member and volunteer marshal who had gone along for the ride with Greg reported condescendingly that the Shark "didn't ask anything." Ben Crenshaw, who had also inspected the par three, "was full of questions," the marshal continued. "But not Greg."

As the October sunlight made a prism of the club's cypress trees, a young man outside the clubhouse, an employee of the club, was giving rides in a golf cart to media members whose cars were parked on the far side of the club property. One such spot was a temporary lot fashioned from one of the holes of the Olympic Club's Ocean Course. Ironically, this particular hole is as far from the Pacific Ocean as any hole on either the Ocean Course or the Lake Course. In fact, it faces the road that runs alongside the lake—Lake Merced—that gives the Lake Course its name. Traffic on that road had been backed up so badly the day before that a few of the players almost missed their tee times. Some people snuck in the back gate.

"You can't come in here," a guard had told one media member.

"But I'm going to lose my job if I'm late," he lied, speaking the universal language of the professional golf tour, which is the language of the hustle.

He got in.

Late in the day, only the main gate, up the driveway from the clubhouse, was still open. To reach it you had to turn around and drive all the way through the manicured course, past endless trees and shrubs, some still flowering this late in the year, up a winding road that ran above the club's tennis courts, closed during tournament week, and out, finally, past a guard who sometimes saluted. To the right, you could detour through the streets of San Francisco all the way downtown. Only a quarter mile from the gate was the turnoff for a parking lot above San Francisco Beach. Hang gliders hovered over the lot and the adjacent bluffs.

It was very windy there, and windier still in the area from which the hang gliders took off. There must have been a dozen riders, some on the ground taking apart their fragile-looking rigs, some still in the air, riding these good winds. One rider had evidently miscalculated his glide, because he was far below on the beach, where he had landed after losing altitude.

"What happened to him?" someone asked a spectator who seemed to be part of the glider crowd.

"He crashed," was the response, in a tone not much different from Billy Glasson's.

A year ago, Greg Norman crashed, right here, a soaring Shark who had landed in the wrong bunker across the highway at the Olympic Club. "That's the demon of Olympic Club," his coach, Butch Harmon, said afterward. When he used the word "demon," Harmon was referring to the apocryphal reason that other, past golfers had unaccountably lost tournaments at Olympic, including Arnold Palmer and Ben Hogan. Of course, Norman's Olympic crash, when he gave away a tournament he should have won to Jim Gallagher, Jr., was not simply the work of the Olympic Club demon.

"Greg made a couple of bad decisions," Butch Harmon admitted sadly.

One of those bad decisions in 1993 had been to hit a sand wedge on the par-five sixteenth hole directly at the flag, which was positioned behind a large bunker. Norman was still winning the tournament at that point; Jim Gallagher, Jr. had already finished his round, and all Norman had to do was par out to clinch victory. On the long sixteenth, unreachable in two, if Norman with his approach had played it safe by shooting toward the left side of the green, and then two-putting for par, he might have won. By trying instead for the birdie, he had made a terrible mental blunder, of the kind that had haunted him in the past. It was as if his ability to think clearly were impeded by some uncontrollable force at moments of pressure or crisis. His detractors would say he choked, but that was far too simple an explanation of his performance. If a demon were at work, it was not a demon of Olympic Club but of Greg Norman.

A year later the memory of this moment was blurred by many other golfing images, including that of a dramatic hole in one by none other than the Shark on the par-three eighth hole at Olympic. Never seriously in the tournament up to that point, Norman had—at least in Billy Glasson's opinion—put himself back into contention with that ace. Afterward, having shot three under for his round, Norman met the media—or, rather, the media met him. More than a dozen reporters cornered him in the locker room, where they had waited while he was in the john, and despite Greg's statement that he now planned to join his wife upstairs for lunch, the questions began, and so, reluctantly, did the answers. Still wearing his hat, the lines on his face looking deep, as if he had to summon a little extra energy to endure another post-game grilling, his monotone betrayed his disappointment. And, soon, his annoyance.

"What was the difference today, Greg?

"I didn't make four bogeys in a row," he said fliply, with a forced smile.

"What did you hit on number eight?"

"Seven-iron. Can't remember the yardage. Hit it perfect. But I have hit a lot of great shots on holes where I made bogey."

"What did you hit for your second shot on one?"

"Three-wood, two hundred and fifty-eight yards."

And so it went, in a scene reminiscent of those in old movies, where a political figure is surrounded by reporters on deadline, each of them hoping for a scoop. With each question Norman further steeled his eyes, staring in derision at his questioner and then looking away in a kind of disgust. The pitch of his voice remained low, not from fatigue but in condescension.

No scoops here, not with this much of a crowd, or the larger assembly that was waiting upstairs in the pressroom, where the Shark, much to his displeasure, had to repeat this verbal performance. Angry afterward at this usurpation of Shark Time, he complained in such strong terms to club officials that they then barred the media from further access to the locker room, in direct violation of PGA Tour rules. Within minutes of Norman's departure, a prissy-voiced man in a suit positioned himself at the outer door. He held a walkie-talkie for communication with the many other guards and workers whose behavior he officiously directed. He might have been a sheriff in charge of an investigation.

Not until tour officials, themselves in possession of walkie-talkies, had fielded complaints from a writer was the matter investigated.

"They can't do that," said the tour's Denise Taylor, whose friendliness could mask the almost built-in suspicion with which she had to meet almost every request. People were always asking her for something. An extra souvenir to take home to the family. A badge for a friend. A better parking spot. And whatever the request, she dealt with it. Shortly, the locker-room door, once again, was opened to the media—this time with an extra guard by the door.

After his long-postponed lunch, the Shark then went to the range, where he hit balls behind the illusory protection of a gallery rope and several ingratiating marshals, one of whom dutifully toted out of a tent a little sign with Norman's name on it that he placed on the ground behind Norman, just like the signs placed behind each of the competitors in this tournament, each of course with the name of the particular contestant, each sign brought out by a marshal only when a particular player was on the range, with the sign then whisked away as soon as the player was done (a necessary precaution, apparently, since virtually anything not nailed down is stolen at these affairs by a public insatiable for evidence of physical contact with Stardom). The ludicrous hypermarketing represented by the signs was pointless in the Shark's case, since there could not have been a person at the tournament who did not know who he was.

Sunday

THE SUN WAS setting over the Pacific. The hang gliders had been out again today. You could see them from the golf course. If they go too far out over the ocean they lose the updraft they need and fall to the water. But if they come too far over land they are not able to get back to the bluffs. To be successful at hang gliding, you need to find and maintain the right balance—just as you do in golf.

Mark McCumber had found it today, beating Fuzzy Zoeller in a one-hole playoff with a forty-foot birdie putt, the longest putt he'd ever made to win a tournament, McCumber said afterward. No, McCumber added patronizingly, he hadn't been playing for the money. McCumber then outlined his immediate plans.

"I won't touch a club in November," he said. In December he would play once, in a team tournament. Ditto January, when he would tee it up for the Mercedes Championships, a boondoggle for the previous year's tournament winners that guaranteed prize money for all the contestants. "Then I won't play again until March," McCumber boasted, never noting what today's $540,000 first prize might have to do with his ability to make such decisions. A contented man who'd been playing on the tour since 1978, McCumber made a special point of recognizing his wife, who sat in the audience at the post-tournament press conference. No one asked her if she had thought about the money.

And no one had the bad manners to ask McCumber or any of the other professional golfers who had competed in the Tour Championship how they would share their good fortune. Was it a source of happiness as well as security? If prize money hadn't been offered this week, would they still have come, like the amateurs and hackers over at Harding Park Golf Course, a public layout past Lake Merced where the tour's San Francisco Open had formerly been contested?

There was no longer a San Francisco Open on the pro tour, but Harding Park hadn't suffered any loss of business. Even at the end of a day in October, the place was booming. And when it was too late to start a round of golf at Harding Park, the driving range still accepted customers. Past a sign in the clubhouse that posted greens fees ("Back 9 B4 7:30 a.m. $10") and across the first tee and down an adjacent path, the range was a narrow chute of land with high netting on either side to keep balls from going astray. The ground there was grassless. Golfers hit off mats.

Back at the Olympic Club, where the initiation fee for members is $42,000, several dozen reporters still lingered, filing stories, drinking beer, making plans for their next rendezvous. Outside in the twilight the first tee beckoned. A fan walked up the first fairway, a par five measuring 533 yards, with a dogleg right from an elevation, so a good drive had to go uphill and either hug the left side of the fairway or fade around the dogleg. Though much of the tournament had been played in the fog, the air today and Saturday had cleared, and it was still clear in the evening. The fan stopped walking when he reached the rise in the fairway. The late-afternoon sunlight shone through the tall trees; the golf holes seemed to cascade downhill like arrangements in a terraced garden. Beyond the first green, past the bluffs above the beach, and over many of the hills of the city of San Francisco loomed the distant, twin towers of the Golden Gate Bridge.

Greg Norman, whose eventual tie for thirteenth place was still good for $71,400 (pocket change), and who even now was flying home to Hobe Sound, Florida, in his personal Gulfstream III—Greg had birdied this hole today, again hitting a three-wood into the green. Had he noticed the bridge? Or were the towers still shrouded in fog at that hour? Did the ineffable mystery of this game lie partly in such trivial questions, or was the explanation of his performance today rooted in something more profound, something that happened to him long ago or even something that had occurred on the PGA Tour (or "out on tour," as most of the players put it, or simply "out here," where according to the tour's inspirational video clips shown weekly on tour telecasts, "Anything's possible")?

That lovely approach on two, when he stuck it to about ten feet, and the putt he then missed, and the pulled tee shot on three, leaving him in that greenside bunker from which he came out too strong, and then the two-putt for bogey to go back to even for the day, and then that awful drive on four, when he pulled his ball into some bushes in the woods above the dogleg and he'd had to punch out from there, three on, two putts, bogey: what happened?

SHARKBITE

YOU HAVE TO experience the downside yourself. That's the best way to give yourself self-confidence. Not a whole lot of people get that in an early stage. It takes a long time to get self-confidence.

If I exude self confidence, it must be in my genes, I don't know. I was a shy, introverted type of kid, self-taught. I could see the writing on the wall about if you wanted to be successful on the golf course, then you have to have this image on the golf course.

I'VE BEEN LUCKY. The trademark, being called the Shark, is going to stick with me all my life. Sometimes I wish I could just be Greg, though. But if I was just Greg, I wouldn't be able to do all the things I want to do. No question about it. You step back because of your family, you want your private time, you want time on your boat without interruptions. Absolutely. But you know, when I started as a kid to play golf, I didn't start out looking for the glory and stardom of it. I went out there to be the best golfer I could be. And whatever came with it, you had to accept it.

IT'S THE HARDEST thing in the world to try to convey how you feel when you make a shot or when you miss one. You can never explain emotions, you can never explain satisfaction. . . . When you're on the golf course, you can't reflect. That's why I like to sit back on a Sunday and reflect. When you reflect on something out there, that's when you lose.

A secret to success is knowing when and how to calm yourself down under extreme conditions. Every athlete has that innate ability to be able to do that. Everybody has a key to their own natural mechanism. Whatever that key is—focusing on your breathing, whistling—it's something you have to do for yourself. Whatever it is, it's individual. When I'm out there, I'm in a zone, unaware of anything else going on about me.

FOLLOWING
THE BALL

ONCE, IN ENDICOTT, New York, which the natives pronounce "Endeecott," a man in the B.C. Open gallery named Paul Tenney was following Brad Faxon around the course. Tenney's then wintertime employee John "Cubby" Burke caddies for Faxon, who was playing in the Endicott tournament, held annually in September, and Cubby was carrying his bag. Tenney runs a ski shop in Sun Valley, Idaho, where Cubby then worked winters. Paul had met Faxon through Cubby; in fact, Faxon had been out to Sun Valley to ski. There was a big trade show for ski people in New York City that Paul was going to, so he'd come early and stopped here to see his friends. It was a Friday afternoon, sunny, in the late fall.

"I love watching these guys play," Paul confessed contentedly. "It's almost as much fun as playing yourself."

If the Olympic Club in San Francisco is not only the most luxurious but perhaps also the most beautifully heartbreaking place to watch professional golf—a suitably grand stage for a performer of such grand dimensions as Greg Norman—then in vivid contrast the most welcoming stop on the PGA Tour is the very public En-Joie course in Endicott, site of the very popular B.C. Open, which takes its name from the cartoon strip created by Broome County resident Johnny Hart. While the exclusive Olympic Club stands high on the dramatic bluffs above San Francisco Beach, its gates guarded, its fragrant fairways protected from outside view by the tall cypress and eucalyptus trees that define its lush grounds, the En-Joie course sits right along Endicott's homey Main Street.

Certainly the lovely surroundings, surreal almost, with a false sense that summer was never going to end, contributed to Paul Tenney's enjoyment of what he was watching, though golf tournaments in the rain, even in a cold rain, were still riveting to see, if not as comfortable. But the real reason for the pleasure Tenney took in the pastoral scene before him lay deep beneath the surface tranquillity of the game and its serene setting.

"There are two distinct kinds of golf—just plain golf and tournament golf," the extraordinary amateur Bobby Jones once wrote. "Golf—the plain variety—is the most delightful of games, an enjoyable, companionable pastime; tournament golf is thrilling, heartbreaking, terribly hard work—a lot of fun when you are young with nothing much on your mind, but fiercely punishing in the end."

Follow the money, they say if you're solving a crime. In tournament golf, as Billy Harmon put it so well at the Olympic Club, you follow the ball.

If you see the ball take off toward the right and then work its way back left, you know the player hit a draw.

Nice shot.

A badly drawn ball is a hook. A badly faded shot is a slice. A fade is a ball that starts left and works its way right.

"You can talk to a fade, but a hook won't listen." Lee Trevino, the man Billy Harmon's father so enjoyed watching, is reputed to have coined that phrase. One of the greatest shotmakers of all time, Trevino in his prime always hit his best shots with some fade. But he could really do whatever he wanted with the ball. He still can, in his fifties and now playing on American professional golf's Senior Tour, a 1980s spinoff from the regular tour that has quickly grown into huge popularity.

The regular professional golf season in this country now extends for ten months; with the addition of several made-for-television and other exhibition events, the golf year truly has no end. The pros pick and choose when they will play, with the more successful, wealthier ones being allowed the luxury of deciding not to play for as many as several months at a time, a choice that might seem strange to the amateur intoxicated with the game but quite in keeping with the spirit of the modern pro's gold standard of achievement.

In the 1990s, Lee Trevino's Senior Tour and the PGA Tour, on which Greg Norman competes, have become an almost weekly television program, with no repeats (until the advent of the Golf Channel). Golf shares longest-season status with professional tennis, but far outstrips tennis in its television coverage, because golf is an advertising demographer's dream, a pressure-filled, high-money-stakes road show whose thrills are used to sell golf clubs and Cadillacs.

Yet golf is the most capricious of games, capable on a regular basis of confounding even the greatest players and of giving grace to the lowliest amateur. And so the golf tour is a confounding place to make a living.

FOLLOW THE BALL:

On the last weekend in March the tour comes to the TPC at Sawgrass, located in Ponte Vedra, south of Jacksonville, Florida. This is the course in the AMEX commercials with architect Pete Dye and golfing star Craig Stadler. But you can't play there during tournament week, even with your AMEX card; not unless your name is on the list of competitors published in such journals as the *Florida Times Union,* which in 1993 printed a daily wraparound half front page devoted to tournament coverage. The last morning's "Special Report" featured a four-color photograph of the German player Bernhard

Langer, paired with Greg Norman on Sunday afternoon. Inside items included a boxed listing of the leaders and a sportswriter's odds for each of them to win. The name in the last line of the list wasn't even playing.

"Brad Faxon," the line began. "Billion-1." And next to those impossible odds was the skinny: "Needs emergency ruling."

Faxon, who the year before had had his best season on tour, was disqualified after the third round for taking an illegal drop on the eighteenth hole. So he returned to his home in Orlando, where he'd spent much of the winter nursing torn rib cartilage suffered in a January skiing accident. At least temporarily that accident had put a stop to the momentum Faxon had generated ever since a tournament he had won the previous summer, a victory that had ultimately turned on a single shot and a single putt. But Faxon seemed unfazed; his primary complaint during the forced layoff had been the inactivity. It was part of his nature, however, not to worry. He was sure his game would come around.

Flying into Jacksonville from the north, you approach one of the large barrier islands that extend along the Atlantic coast from Florida all the way to Hilton Head and Cape Hatteras off the Carolinas. Low over the water, suddenly you cross directly over Amelia Island and Fernandina Beach, the blue ocean and the Intracoastal Waterway framing the island's lush green. It seems lusher than it should, long strips of green laid out in patterns with little splotches of whitish brown the color of the condo roofs along Amelia Beach or adjacent to it. They poke through treetops, and if the day is hot and you live in the north you may think of the green when your plane lands and taxis past palm trees.

This is where the pros travel to make money every March. By a curb outside the airport one of them was standing, a late arrival whose face looked familiar from television. He was putting his clubs into the trunk of a white Buick, which he'd drive all week for free. A courtesy car, which he'd park each day in his own courtesy parking space, next to the TPC club-house, each space marked by a small sign with a pro's name on it, and the choicest spaces, the ones closest to the clubhouse, reserved for past winners of the tournament. A row of winners' parking places starting at the bottom of the stairs that lead to the clubhouse. The very first space reserved for last year's winner.

Davis Love III.

One of the longest hitters in a sport obsessed with length, Love is the son of a professional golfer, Davis Love II, who went on to become a successful golf teacher. When he was a boy, Davis Love III used to accompany his father to the very tournaments in which he now competed. But his father was not here. He had died in the crash of a small plane he was taking back to the barrier island off the coast of Georgia where he was the teaching pro, and where his son still lives with his wife and young children. A college schoolmate and close friend of Michael Jordan's—he taught Jordan golf—Love unfortunately comes across to many golf fans as unsmiling and aloof. With a seriousness of purpose that often manifests itself as a scowl, he looks unhappy, even unfriendly, whereas, like so many athletes thrown into the spotlight, he is simply shy.

Love had driven in his four-wheel-drive pickup truck from Sea Island to the tournament, whose official name was The Players Championship. The truck had an oversize cab, spacious enough to hold Love's enormous golf bag. Late Wednesday afternoon, the day before the tournament began, the truck was parked in Love's honorary place, because Love was on the course, at the first tee, where he and fellow touring pro Rocco Mediate were about to do some p.r. for the tour, giving a kids' golf clinic, sponsored by Coca-Cola.

The area around the tee had been turned into an amphitheater through the use of banked railroad ties, a trademark of architect Dye. In the ten years since the course opened, rain had washed any residue of tar from the wood, which had also been dried by the wind and sun, the wind that blew through the palm trees that rimmed the amphitheater, the sun that shone over those same swaying palms, which made shadows on the tee but didn't keep the sun from shining directly on the people sitting on the tiered seats.

The design, part of a concept called stadium golf, made for excellent spectator viewing. Other uses of the railroad ties, particularly to buttress pond banks, created shot values. Some shots became more difficult simply because of the unpredictable bounces a ball could take off a railroad tie or because of the awkward stance the proximity of a tie could cause a player.

This late afternoon a cloud cover in northern Florida shaded direct sunlight. In fact, the forecast said it might rain tomorrow for the first round of the tournament. Earlier in the month it had rained very hard during a storm that left the Northeast buried in snow, and in the aftermath of that rain the wind blew trees down and made a mess of the course. But the grounds crew, as the television announcers were forever saying, had worked so hard and well that the grass was a late-spring green, the fairways still a little muddy in spots but with only sporadic bare spots. A crowd gathered to sit in the four-o'clock cloudy warmth, listening to Davis and Rocco explain the golf swing to children. From a marketing standpoint, the target audience of that event was really the parents, but the kids in their free red-and-white Coke visors were having a good time.

"Hold your finish," said Davis Love, looking spiffy and comfortable in cream-colored pants. He was hitting a pitching wedge, but he soon switched to a six-iron, then a four-iron. With each swing the ball sailed smoothly into the air and went an immense distance. Yet Love looked as if he was expending very little physical energy.

The wide arc of Love's swing, with its long, full extension as he took the club back and its smooth, powerful impact with the ball as he brought the club through the hitting area, and then the follow-through, with its audible "thwish" made by the speed of the clubhead and shaft moving through the air, was based on body mechanics so complicated that an entire subindustry of books and videos and live teachers has been built upon their elucidation.

An immense number of products have been designed to turn the hacker into a smooth swinger. The seductive illusion "I can do this" is based on the fact that every once in a while even the hacker does indeed hit a shot that a professional wouldn't sneer at.

Love hit a ball with his driver.

"Same swing," he said.

The ball disappeared past the long waste bunker on the right side of the fairway and came to rest more than three hundred yards away. Most of that distance had been carried, Love's ball flying up and out on an elliptical trajectory and coming to rest after a soft bounce and brief roll.

"Now, the first thing you should do when you play golf is ... tie your shoes." The laces on one of Love's had come untied. His remark prompted light laughter. Next, he and Rocco invited some of the kids to try what they had been doing. The first boy, barely taller than his club, hit his ball perhaps a hundred yards. This was quite a poke, a feat almost in scale with Love's drive, and the crowd applauded. The kid beamed.

The water surface of a small pond on the other side of the amphitheater, hard by the hill leading up to the clubhouse, lay still. But along the much larger pond that bordered the eighteenth fairway, across the large lawn that lay between the clubhouse and driving range, several other players were fishing, including another of the game's premier players, Corey Pavin.

Anyone who consults the PGA Tour's annual media guide, with its records and bios of the golfers who are exempt from having to qualify for a particular year's tournaments, in the category for each golfer called "Special Interests," which merits top billing right after "Family and College," will find in case after case, sometimes to the exclusion of any other special interest, this activity: "Fishing."

Of course many players listed other special interests, ranging from David Ogrin's incongruous "Christianity" to Steve Lowery's all-inclusive "Sports," which was also Michael Bradley's, Dudley Hart's, and Greg Kraft's only special interest. Billy Andrade, Jay Haas, Scott Hoch, John Huston, Brian Kamm, Billy Mayfair, Jim McGovern, Andy North, and Howard Twitty amended this to "All Sports." Reported the tour's long driver and sometime *cause célèbre* John Daly: "Most Sports"; while Loren Roberts's sole special interest was, astonishingly, "Golf."

The late-afternoon golfer-fishermen, whose practice of their special interest here might strike some observers as an odd way of getting away from the game, lingered into the dinner hour. "How is it?" shouted a young fan to Bruce Lietzke as Lietzke left the lake and walked back toward the palatial, pagoda-like clubhouse.

A tour veteran, the successful Lietzke is known as much for the relatively little effort he seems to expend on his game as for his golfing prowess. He regularly takes off a month or two at a time to watch his kids' Little League games, to be at home—and, of course, to fish. Indeed, Lietzke lists two special interests in his life, one of them racing cars and the other "Serious Fishing."

Tour legend has it that Lietzke's caddie, himself unable to believe that Lietzke did not even practice golf during his long breaks from the game, hid a banana in the head cover of Lietzke's driver after the last round of the last tournament before one of Lietzke's breaks. Several weeks later when Lietzke returned to the tour his caddy checked the head cover of the driver. The banana, or its rotten remains, was still there.

Now Lietzke looked up at the fan who was calling to him and said without breaking stride, "Not bad." These were his only words before he disappeared beyond a door guarded by a man who carefully checked trespassers, defined as the general public, for the proper admittance badge.

On a practice putting green between the pond and driving range, Paul Azinger rolled putt after putt smoothly into the hole. Ten years before, Azinger had come here as a marginal, twenty-three-year-old player trying to qualify for exempt status on the tour. He had so little money that he and his wife, Toni, lived out of a mobile trailer, on the road and at home. He could not afford a caddy the week of that qualifying tournament and instead carried his clubs in a cart. The only fan who followed him around during those six torturous days was Toni. One of her husband's playing partners, Brad Faxon, was also attempting to earn the badge—in actuality, a money clip—that would permit him entry in PGA Tour tournaments for the coming year. Brad Faxon and Paul Azinger played together the last two rounds in that qualifying tournament, universally called a school (as in Qualifying School, Q-School, or tour school), and Toni watched every shot. The exempt status her husband earned at the 1983 tour school he subsequently lost, requiring him to qualify again. Then, suddenly and mysteriously, his game clicked, and in only a few years he was elected by his peers Golfer of the Year. He was a star, with career earnings that soon put him near the top of the all-time list.

PGA TOUR HEADQUARTERS are located a good pitching-wedge shot from the green of the first hole of the Tournament Players Club at Ponte Vedra. Until he stepped down as commissioner after twenty years in 1994, Deane Beman presided over his empire from a spacious office at the farthest remove from the building's entrance. A former tour player, with four victories to his credit, Beman was also twice the United States Amateur champion—the same title that the loudly heralded Tiger Woods would capture in 1994 and 1995. Beman left his job, which paid him in the seven figures, to return to competition as a senior player. But he didn't have enough career money to be exempt, and he failed to qualify during the senior qualifying school held in the fall after his retirement as commissioner. The only way he would be able to enter senior tournaments was via sponsor exemptions.

As Beman knew only too well, success as a golfer, whether on the regular tour or as a senior, required not only physical skill but also "something inside." Those were his words, and he reflected on them when he was still commissioner. Never a glad-hander, Beman could come across as almost reticent in casual conversation, but his observations about golfers were astute and unhampered by false sentiment. Watching warmups on the practice range, Beman said, he could easily and accurately make judgments about the faults and virtues of different players' swings.

"But how can they perform in competition?" he asked. "You know, there are no substitutes in golf. On the tour, you've got to be able to perform in turmoil and tranquillity. If you can't, you shouldn't stay."

They were words he might have heeded in 1995 when, though leading in driving accuracy, after competing in twenty-six Senior Tour events, he had won $137,960, good for a distant sixty-second place on the money list.

TO DEAL WITH the pressure of their inscrutable profession, Tom Kite and Paul Azinger and every other successful golf professional wear a mask. Veteran Raymond Floyd's swagger suggests a prima donna; crowd favorite and former U.S. Open champion Fuzzy Zoeller acts and talks the part of a joker; for years Lee Trevino has cultivated an outgoing, colorful character known as SuperMex, yet away from the course he is withdrawn. Phil Mickelson seems to be one of Fred MacMurray's three sons, while Brad Faxon comes across as the good neighbor (but you might get the feeling over a barbecue in the backyard that you shouldn't invite him to play poker, that behind that innocent grin he is calculating what it will take to beat you). The better a man's

mask, the better his odds at succeeding in a world whose uni-
formly upbeat, genial demeanor belies its cutthroat, hustler's
heart, a game Lee Trevino said he learned by making bets for
more money than he had in his pocket.

To excel at professional golf is lonely work; you have no
teammates to help you or hide your mistakes. And you have
to combine many traits and abilities. You have to be strong to
drive the ball far but gentle to have the right touch or feel
around the greens. You have to be able to concentrate for long
stretches of time in an outdoor environment filled with distractions. You have to remember subtle contours of a green,
what a ball will do when putted with or against different grains
of grass, how varying temperatures affect the feel of your golf
ball. And you constantly have to forget the failures that are
built into the game while avoiding excessive pride when you
temporarily overcome them.

"Golf fears—worries about trouble to the right or left, fear
of pulling the ball, that sort of thing," preoccupy players, confessed former tour star Frank Beard, now a senior golfer and
golf broadcaster.

"My swing is technically sound, but my tempo is thrown off
by these dark images I have. I get over the ball and there's a
pervading fear. I try to focus on the positive: 'Where do I want
the ball to go?' But I get a message back: 'Oh, jeez, I don't want
it to go over there.' Once you start that, you're dead. Almost
invariably you wind up hitting it right where your fears are
leading you."

Constant anxiety epitomizes this choke sport. It is a tension
borne of each individual pro's knowledge that with the very
next shot or putt he could lose it all, never again making a
penny as a traveling, tournament professional. In fact, this very
thing has happened many times. Scott Verplank, the hot young
prospect of the late 1980s, plunged to 266th place on the annual
money list in 1991, and then in 1992 fell further, to 309th out of
321. Verplank's problems started with a bad shoulder, which

eventually healed, but no such reason could explain the monumentally long swoon of Tom Watson, once the finest player in the world.

The last golfer to dominate the tour for an extended period (late 1970s to early 1980s), Watson has had only one PGA Tour win since 1984. Many people believed Watson's relative decline might be traced to his second-place finish to Seve Ballesteros in that year's British Open. He had already won the prestigious tournament five times and was poised for a sixth when his second shot on the seventeenth hole went past the green and over an adjacent road, where it came to rest next to a wall. He took bogey.

Of course, Watson still commands attention on the golf course; much of it, alas, is negative. He moves more quickly than almost any other player on tour, taking very little time to set himself up for each swing and striding impatiently from shot to shot. Some of the men who play with him, particularly the younger ones who did not witness his greatness, make fun of his terrible putting. And they accuse him of being obstinate and selfish, qualities that may have served him well when they were hidden by his success but that now provoke derision. Though he is one of the most financially successful players in tour history, he hasn't bought a fleet of expensive cars or moved his family to a mansion in Florida, where more pro golfers live than anywhere else. In fact, staying near his boyhood hometown around Kansas City, he actually puts away his golf clubs for a while each winter, as though aware that the professional game's perpetual warm weather is false at the core, an affront to the sport's historic roots and out of sync with the seasonal rhythm of life as he knows it. And he is also not afraid of controversy, resigning from the Kansas City Country Club in protest over discrimination in its membership policies. He refused to play in the Sun City Million Dollar Challenge. But somehow even these acts come across as self-serving, and his response to the success of others can seem resentful.

Players can be harsh in their response. Two of them practicing their short games after playing with Watson one day tried to imitate his putting stroke. And they gossiped with a third pro about the way Watson had upbraided them for playing too slowly (a charge that, in this case, was unfair).

"What is it about him?" one of them asked. "He's turning into a dick."

In his preface to Watson's book about chipping and putting, Jack Nicklaus wrote prophetically, "Someday maybe he'll start missing some short putts and come back to the real world." This book was published in 1983, the year after Watson beat Nicklaus and won the U.S. Open with a chip (also on the seventeenth hole). Many called it greatest shot in the history of golf when, with his ball nestled in the rough behind the green, Watson would have been lucky to get onto the green and two-putt.

Now, hitting the ball better than ever, Watson could no longer make the crucial putts. The strain of his slump showed in the way he clasped his folded arms tightly as he talked, in the purse of his lips, and in the somber tone with which he discussed his golfing failure. Handsome and rugged, his bulging forearms and freckled face well tanned, he frequently referred to himself in the third person, as if he were a doctor discussing a very sick patient. But he was his own patient and he hadn't yet found a cure (though he'd hired his old caddy back and resumed a rigorous practice schedule). In a word, Watson had what golfers call the yips, a mysterious nervous twitch that undermines a golfer's ability to make a short putt. Unlike Bernhard Langer, who cured cases of the yips by adopting an unorthodox grip, or Ben Crenshaw, whose smooth stroke has never been perceptibly impacted as he has grown older, Watson even had poor posture when he bent over a three-footer, his shoulders hanging limply rather than naturally, his arms bent awkwardly.

The prospect of making a single poor putt was constantly on Watson's mind, as it is for every pro golfer, because the

margin between winning and losing in this ancient, tantaliz-
ing, testing game is so exceedingly small: a statistical difference of hundredths of a putt per hole could mean a difference
of hundreds of thousands of dollars in annual earnings. More
than simple fear of temporary failure, the anxiety of a pro
golfer turns on the ever-present nightmare of complete break-
down.

Every week during the ten-month-long PGA Tour season,
the career money list is updated at tour headquarters in Ponte
Vedra, where the Players Championship was being contested.
Ten years ago, $1 million in career earnings would have placed
a golfer among an elite of just forty-two men. Nowadays, with
the inflation of purses, that amount doesn't even put a player
among the top hundred.

The odds of making it are also poor for a newcomer. Of the
850 men who would attempt to qualify for their tour cards in
1995, only the top forty and ties were successful. And there
were thousands of other golfers who wanted to be among those
contestants but were not good enough or, as is often the case
in golf, did not play up to their capabilities when it really mat-
tered. Most of the golfers against whom Brad Faxon competed
at qualifying school in 1983 were off the tour, unable to cross
what Paul Azinger calls the "fine line" between success and
failure. In the entire history of golf, only thirteen men have won
at least six major tournaments (counting both the United States
Amateur and British Amateur as majors; the others, commonly
used in today's tabulations, are the Masters, the United States
and British Opens, and the PGA).

What distinguishes a top player is the ability to keep his
game together and his head focused shot after shot after shot
in a game that militates against this.

"Playing out here on tour is a matter of making the right cor-
rections," explained Bill Glasson, who first qualified for the
tour the same year as Azinger and Faxon but, like Azinger, had
to requalify the following year after winning only $17,845 his

first season. The players who are successful, Glasson believes, are those who learn to make the necessary adjustments.

In any given week, most of the men on tour fail this assignment. Over time, the consistent failures leave the tour. On average, just four to six new players a year survive. This is an incredibly tiny total.

The survivors, men like the hard-willed Lanny Wadkins or the demonstrative "Walrus," Craig Stadler, have learned to perform when they are not at their best. Or, according to Glasson, have realized that peak performance is an illusion, because there is always something about your swing to work on, to be concerned about.

"I have never felt good about it," Glasson confesses. "Every day you have to tweak something."

THE PLAYERS CHAMPIONSHIP is one of the richest tournaments of the PGA Tour season, and winning it also carries a ten-year tour exemption, meaning the player is automatically entitled to enter all tour events for the next decade. Nick Price was leading after three rounds in 1993, but only a stroke back were three men, including Greg Norman.

Close friends off the course, Price and Norman could not be more different on it. The only physical feature the two men share is a prominent nose, but Norman's is hawklike while Price's is wider and more flattened. In contrast to Norman's blond hair, swept back to reveal the beginning of baldness above his forehead, Price's brown hair looks perpetually as if it has just come from under the blow dryer, with several unmanageable hairs sticking out over the top. At six feet one, an inch taller than Price, Norman also boasts a slightly flatter belly and more muscular forearms, which he shows off by wearing brightly colored shirts and tight pants. Unhurried as he plays golf, spending an inordinate amount of time over each shot, Norman is the consummate deliberator during a round, whereas Price is more instinctual, his stroke itself much quicker, almost jablike. Nick also smokes occasionally as he plays, away from the television lens, whereas Norman snacks on fruit (and afterward drinks beer).

The Shark had shot a solid 68 the day before. At Doral, earlier that month, he'd been in an even better position, though that hadn't stopped the kind of carping that seemed to accompany him wherever and however he played.

At the first hole in the final Doral round, Norman had a six-shot lead over Paul Azinger. When Norman stepped to the tee, back in the clubhouse the early finishers were talking among themselves about the Shark's chances. He'd lose it, many of the players said. He couldn't keep this going. Twenty-one under par for three rounds. That was some kind of golf, even if the conditions were benign. But he wasn't going to continue. No way, agreed the men who in 1990 when Norman was first on the money list voted instead for Wayne Levi as Player of the Year. Wayne Levi! Wayne won four tournaments that year, but he wasn't in Norman's class; he would never have the staying power of Norman, never have the ability to dominate his profession over a long period of time. The golf he played was methodical, technically sound, and driven by a fierce competitiveness, but ultimately workmanlike. Norman said he didn't take being snubbed by his peers personally—it wasn't the first time, nor, certainly, the last—but the following year he was winless and had his worst season since 1983, the year he joined the American tour. Almost another year passed before he won again. Now, in Florida in early March of 1993, he was leading at Doral, but out of his earshot his peers whispered what they knew he'd do.

Choke.

Having secured his first tour win in two years at the Canadian Open the previous September, Norman was embarking on a "seven-year plan" to reassert his place as the top golfer in the world, a ranking he had at that time lost to the likes of Nick Faldo and Fred Couples. At Doral, only the second tournament of the year he'd entered, he arrived each day in royal style by helicopter (to the envy of his fellow pros), instantly identifiable in his designer clothes with their shark insignias. He did not buckle under the pressure, instead setting a tournament scoring record on his way to victory. Then the tour worked its way north, along and near the Atlantic coast, to the TPC at Ponte Vedra. What lurked in the dangerous waters, what specters of past disaster or excellence waited to haunt or inspire the Shark or his prey?

IN ALL OF professional sports, there is probably nothing more terrifying—or thrilling—than hitting a drive or a putt on which winning or losing one of the world's major golf tournaments depends. Nor is there anything sadder than the sight of such a shot landing in a pond, or of a putt kissing the cup's lip. Nothing sadder, that is, except seeing your opponent's lucky shot land where even he might not have reasonably expected it to go: into the hole.

People are always posing questions about this to Greg Norman—"the toothless shark," his detractors still deride him, whose greatness sometimes seems to lie in his one defect: always on the attack, he lacks the ability to lay back. People quiz him incessantly about the sinking feeling when Larry Mize beat him in the 1986 Masters with a chip-in or the next year when Bob Tway did the same thing with a bunker shot on the last hole of the PGA. Or the 1989 British Open when he beat himself, driving his ball into a bunker no one else had reached on the last playoff hole. A look of controlled rage will come over his handsome face, the skin deeply tanned and the still-golden blond hair falling over a brow lined with the first wrinkles of approaching middle age (he would turn forty in 1995), and as he grits those perfect white teeth the usual smile turns ever so briefly to a scowl, as it did after he lost to Nick Faldo the previous December in Jamaica, three months before the Tournament Players Championship. But by then, Norman had become a grinder, working with a new coach on a revamped swing and putting in long hours of highly purposeful practice at the range.

When the Shark was at the golf course no one initiated small talk with him, even on the practice tee in Ponte Vedra. On that range, all the competitors hit beautiful shots, or so it seemed as ball after ball sailed on strikingly similar, perfect parabolas into the horizon. The ability to hit those terrific shots in a real round, under the pressure of competition, defined the difference between success and failure in a tournament, according to the conventional wisdom.

But anyone watching Greg Norman hitting golf balls on the TPC range and then comparing what he did to the efforts of others might conclude that the conventional wisdom belied a deeper reality. Even on the range, the Shark hit the ball more consistently on target, with greater distance or touch, depending on what was called for, than most of the other golfers on tour. In comparison to most of his peers he was, in a word, *better.* Former star and now NBC golf commentator Johnny Miller believed Norman was the finest driver of the ball in golf history. Here on the range, Greg Norman was in his element, and he knew it. So did everyone else around him, including his caddy, Tony Navaro, who protectively told interlopers that Greg was "in his office," a clichéd expression used by athletes in many sports.

Most pro golfers at such times carry on a disjointed, staccato conversation to relieve the monotony and tension of their labor. But Norman usually hit balls by himself in virtual isolation at the empty end of the range. Only Tony and one of his competitors were closer than the distance of a chip-in from just off a small green. Away from the Shark, sucking one morning on cigarettes and trading jokes with other golfers, NBC announcers Roger Maltbie and Bob Trumpy passed the time more nervously than the athletes who were the ostensible stars of the show. Maltbie, himself a tour player, ingratiatingly laughed at "Trump's" Ken Green pun. Green wore shoes and gloves dyed the color of his name.

"Gangrene," quipped Trump.

"Yeah!" said Maltbie. "That's what you should put on your family Christmas cards. 'From the gang Green.' Send it to everyone on your list."

"There are only two names on the list," responded the golfer Commissioner Beman had fined more than anyone else on tour, usually for what Beman deemed inappropriate language. Many of Green's fines were for throwing clubs. Several times he has thrown putters into lakes and was fined for doing so.

"And yours is one of them, Roger," Green said at the TPC.

If he had heard any of this boys' banter, Norman didn't let on. Gradually going from short to mid to long irons and then woods, he methodically hit shot after shot, the only sound the crisp click of clubhead to ball and Tony's occasional, supportive, sweet-voiced "Nice one, Greg."

The media often portrays Norman as a character out of an old-time Hollywood movie. And he obligingly acts the part, once winning a tournament to which he'd invited a young cancer victim as his guest and presenting the tournament trophy to the boy. But for every such story of thoughtfulness there was another about how thin the Shark's skin was.

Once, with a score to settle after a six-week hiatus from the tour, Norman held court near the entrance to the media tent. The area was cordoned off from the public but still crowded with reporters and photographers. It was a hot afternoon after a long day of slow play. A week before, attempting to disparage Greg humorously, a writer covering another tournament had alluded to Norman's reputation for losing tournaments on the last hole. The Shark had taken it personally, and now, while Chris Berman waited to interview him for ESPN, the most glamorous star on the tour started complaining about the media, most of whose members earned less money than Tony Navaro. A print reporter, near Berman's side, faced Norman and nodded.

"I was there," he said obsequiously in reference to the earlier event. "I was *at* that tournament."

The Shark directed his blue eyes at the reporter. With one hand he removed from his head the black straw Stetson with its Shark insignia and with the other hand brushed the sweat from his deeply tanned forehead. His beautiful hair seemed not just blond but golden. He listened gratefully to the reporter, as if the man were speaking to him on cue.

"Yeah, that's right, Greg. That wasn't fair, what they wrote."

Norman bought things compulsively, the press reported (much to the Shark's displeasure). Another Ferrari or yacht. Not long ago, the story goes, he passed an opulent place in Florida that his wife, Laura, a former airlines flight attendant, said she loved. So he knocked on the door and made an offer, on the spot, to the startled owner.

"That's a pile of crap," Norman said later about the story. But he had bought a new house, where he lives with Laura and their two children about eighty days a year, sometimes for a few weeks in a row, longer than he stays anywhere else at a stretch. It may be one of the few places in the world he can feel completely at ease. On the road he is followed everywhere. At Augusta, Georgia, where the Masters is played every year, he rents a house during tournament week; many of the players do this. But when Laura Norman wants to run errands, her husband has to stay in the car because his presence in a store causes such a stir. He is immediately surrounded by people who want his autograph, ask him how it felt to lose to Fuzzy Zoeller in the 1984 U.S. Open, remind him that when Nicklaus won that 1986 Masters at the age of forty-six he, Norman, would have been in a playoff had it not been for a bogey on the last hole. His most passionate fans are emboldened to confront him physically. At the Tour Championship a fan tried to trip him as he left the range.

At that same tournament, one of the people following Norman was a woman in red pants who was also wearing a black straw hat with the Shark insignia on it. She was the wife of coach Butch Harmon, who was also following Greg, and they held hands as they walked. Later, Laura Norman, denied entrance at the door to the clubhouse near one of the practice putting greens, smiled and said to the attendant, who had not recognized her: "Okay, we'll go around to the front." And she did. It was the kind of small, everyday incident that never publicly takes place in her husband's life.

At home, however, the Shark can get up before dawn and work in the office that is not far from the pool, dressed only in shorts and a shirt. Or practice his short game; there's a full-size putting green in the yard. Or he can run down the road to the new course he owns, codesigned with TPC architect Pete Dye. He can pick up the kids from school, eschewing one of his Ferraris for a Chevy Suburban. Maybe, if the parents of his daughter's friends will respect his privacy, he can watch her soccer practice. Born in 1982, she's a good athlete. In his celebrity isolation from the daily world, nothing gives Morgan-Leigh's famous father greater happiness than to follow her around on the golf course as her caddy.

SHARKBITE

HOW YOU DO is not the intervention of fate, it's the nature of the game of golf or any sport in general. You look at any of the best quarterbacks in the world. One game they can be looking fantastic because the wide receivers are catching everything; the next game, it's the same sort of pass but the wide receivers aren't that good so the quarterback looks like he's not throwing as well. The same goes with golf. Even more so because it's an individual sport. You play an offensive and defensive game in one. You've got to be on the attack; you've got to be mentally sharp, physically sharp, your game's got to be sharp. There's about four or five different sections of your game that need to be right. I don't think fate has anything to do with it. Fate is the result when a golf ball hits a tree and it goes out of bounds. Or you can hit a good shot, one that lands on the green but bounces over in the back bunker and you make five from that point.

HOW TO WIN
A GOLF
TOURNAMENT

STATISTICS CAN BE misleading, but of the fewer than two hundred players on tour who annually complete at least fifty rounds, the difference between the best putter and the worst is slightly more than a tenth of a putt per hole. Yet the resulting difference in winnings helps make men such as Greg Norman millionaires and forces others to get a club pro job.

A poor putter can partially overcome that deficiency—but only partially—by being especially strong in some other facet of the game. And some players seem to defy statistically driven odds.

Brad Faxon among them.

A somewhat short yet inaccurate driver, Faxon has a short game that most players would kill for. He's one of the best putters in golf, and he excels at such facets of golf as sand saves (getting out of a sand bunker in one shot and then sinking the putt, or simply holing the bunker shot). But the real explanation for his success is elusive. Proficiency at golf, especially golf at this very high level, is not just tension-filled. It is also puzzling.

In looks or game, Faxon would never be mistaken for Norman. Though he drives his Infiniti too fast, favors a classic wardrobe, and lets his sandy red hair grow to his shirt collar, Faxon is not glamorous. Only his energy level is on a par with Norman's, and Brad invests it differently. He doesn't practice nearly as much, at least not at tournaments, where Norman seems to use the range as a refuge from the public. He plays more quickly than Norman; he also leaves the course sooner, to be with his wife and children, to hang out with friends. A screenwriter friend from Los Angeles comes to all the West Coast tournaments, and Brad usually spends some time with him afterward. They have been talking about making a movie together.

Through 1991, Faxon had won only two tournaments, one of which in the sometimes arcane regulations of the tour wasn't even counted as an "official" win until a subsequent policy change. Then, in a span of just a few weeks in 1992, Faxon's golfing life had changed dramatically. He won twice, narrowly missed winning a third, and with his other earnings for the year suddenly found himself ranked among the top ten golfers on the entire American tour. He won almost $1 million on the golf course. Elected by his peers to the tour's policy board and elevated by one of his former sponsors, Titleist, to be an advertising spokesman, Brad Faxon was becoming a "name."

The day after returning home from his last important golf tournament of the season, Faxon was itching to get out on his roller blades. As a kid growing up in Rhode Island, he'd played some ice hockey. And he still skated whenever he could—which wasn't often, since he lived in Florida at the moment. Lived there, that is, when he wasn't traveling around the country playing professional golf, which he did for most of the year. During one summer stretch he'd been on the road ten consecutive weeks, though part of that time was spent with old friends and family in Cape Cod, where his grandfather used to run a course. So going to the Cape was a kind of homecoming, too.

This homecoming with his wife, Bonnie, and their two young

daughters was different. There would be months together without so much travel. Two months if you didn't count the trip to Bermuda for the workshop sponsored by Titleist, which Brad had been endorsing since he turned professional almost ten years ago. Or the time he'd spend working on his game with his present swing doctor, Jim McClean, who taught at the Doral resort in Miami during the winter, and whose other pupils included Peter Jacobsen and golf's then all-time leading money winner, Tom Kite. And there were the two weekends he'd play in unofficial events, the mixed team tournament in early December, with partner Betsy King, and the Johnnie Walker World Championship in Jamaica just before Christmas. After that his schedule was carefully mapped out. He knew exactly where he'd be in early January: at the Tournament of Champions.

The year he came on tour, 1984, Brad was expected to succeed. He had won the Fred Haskins trophy, golf's equivalent of football's Heismann Trophy while at Furman University, where he was twice an All-American in golf, and after his 1983 graduation he competed for the United States in the prestigious Walker Cup. While holding on to his playing card, sometimes precariously, every year since he turned pro, Faxon had to contend with a constant question: why aren't you winning? The questioning did not really end until one summer day in 1992 at Pleasant Valley Country Club in Worcester, Massachusetts.

ONE HUNDRED AND *forty-eight to the pin. One hundred and forty-eight over water to a putt that could win the tournament. One hundred and forty-eight . . .*

Brad Faxon had known the yardage before Cubby told him. Every day that week on this hole, the par-four seventeenth, he'd hit a two-iron off the tee, and now he'd hit a two-iron his former teacher Joe Benevento would later call a career-changing shot. Though he got less distance with that club than he would have with a wood, Faxon still hit it an astounding 245 yards. That made the distance 167 yards to the center of the green. All week, his two-irons on this hole had left him in the middle of the fairway. That's why he'd hit that club: with more loft than his driver or three-wood, it was more accurate, and this fairway was relatively narrow, guarded by trees on both sides, with the landing area not visible over a knoll from the tee.

Today's pin in this fourth and final round had been moved up front, closer to Faxon.

Closer to the pond, too.

If he hit the ball in the pond like so many others before him, he'd have to take a drop, losing another shot. Even Tom Watson, who was winning the first of his five British Opens when Faxon was in junior high school, had dunked one at this hole a few years back. With the subsequent penalty stroke the best score a golfer could hope for unless he holed his next shot was a bogey five.

Brad Faxon needed four. A par. And then another par on the eighteenth if he was finally going to capture a prize that had eluded him for over a decade. It was late on a summer Sunday afternoon at Pleasant Valley. Faxon had a one-stroke lead over the young phenom Phil Mickelson. But Mickelson was done for the day; he'd already posted his score.

"It's a hard nine," whispered Cubby, referring to the club he thought Brad should select. Cubby's blond hair was streaked with sweat, because he'd been carrying Brad's fifty-pound bag since midday. People called him Cubby because his size and blond hair had once reminded someone of Jack Nicklaus, whose nickname was the Golden Bear. A semipro hockey player in the winter, Cubby had big forearms and the same forceful attitude that outwardly characterizes Faxon and most of the golfers with whom Faxon competes.

Lanky and angular, Faxon was sweating just like Cubby as the Pleasant Valley tournament neared its conclusion. Not counting his swings on the practice range that morning, he had taken exactly sixty-one strokes today, a little less than half of them putts. He could take eight more strokes and still preserve his one-stroke margin over Mickelson, the only golfer left in the field who could beat him, the young man just out of college whom people were calling the latest, "next Nicklaus." Mickelson had tremendous power that seemed to come from nowhere; watching him hit a ball, an observer might conclude he was spending far less effort than he would to comb his neatly cut hair. And Mickelson already possessed something of a top pro's aura on the golf course, the ability to communicate a nonverbal message of supreme confidence and command. This quality, which Greg Norman exudes playing golf, is a sixth athletic sense, a kind of cockiness, something that many players never acquire completely. But for all those who do, it is equivalent to having a proverbial extra club in their golf bags, intimidating to opponents. Though he is almost ten years Mickelson's senior, Faxon, at Pleasant Valley, was still searching for it; sometimes he was close to it, sometimes not. This day it was waiting to be claimed somewhere beyond the pond.

Faxon focused on the imaginary flight of his ball to the green, which at such moments could seem shockingly small. And then, in a split second, the pond could become in a golfer's mind a lake. But Faxon tried to imagine only the result of his next shot, the place on the green where he wanted his ball to land, just past the flagstick.

If Faxon got more of his approach shot than he wanted and the ball went too far, he could be in trouble where the gallery had trampled the grass or, worse, where some trees hid a brook, the very brook that fed the pond. A soft nine-iron would certainly land in the pond.

"One hundred and forty-eight, eh, Cubby?"

"One hundred and forty-eight."

Nervously, Faxon picked a piece of grass off the ground and threw it up into the warm, still summer air. The grass fell to the ground.

I don't know why I'm playing so well. I don't want to think about why. I just want to do it.

Staring across the pond to the seventeenth green, Faxon could have recalled his three-wood shot under similar circumstances at the San Diego tournament a few years earlier. That much longer shot on the eighteenth hole, a par five at Torrey Pines, required him to come over some trees, then a long expanse of fairway, and finally a pond. Though he needed a birdie to have a chance at winning, he'd elected to lay up. The risk had seemed too great.

As he deliberated about what to do at Pleasant Valley, Faxon forgot his family, who were watching him from the other side of the gallery ropes, and all those hometown friends from Rhode Island who had come to watch him that day, hundreds of them cheering his entire round. They defined their connection with Faxon in endearingly tenuous ways. One young man from Smithfield, Rhode Island, boasted he had "played *against* Brad in high school." Some of Faxon's closest friends had been walking rounds with him here since the first time he was invited to play in this tournament as a college student and had been the only amateur in the field to make the cut.

But none of them, even the most knowledgeable, knew what it was like to be in his shoes on the seventeenth fairway. What he loved about golf was the precision with which you could attempt to make a shot, knowing that perfection was nevertheless impossible. At Pleasant Valley, Faxon tried to shut out everything in his life but the next shot, which was so like thousands of shots he had hit since he was a boy, aiming one-irons from his backyard at a sailboat moored offshore in Narragansett Bay. So like all those shots in their physical mechanics yet so different in scenario.

Paul Azinger once revealed that he didn't start winning pro tournaments until he learned to breathe. Breathing calmly at Pleasant Valley, Brad was wearing his red "Mindset" shirt, which the ubiquitous sports psychologist Dr. Bob Rotella—

whose client list seems to include every man on tour—had convinced him would conjure a "bold, aggressive attitude." (Faxon, who paid Dr. Rotella for his services, was paid for promoting these shirts.) Rotella, who believes "a golfer can and must decide how he will think," would even include among his future clients Greg Norman, who in 1995 would reveal that he had talked to Dr. Bob.

Faxon stared again at the green. To a stranger, he looked like he might be deciding what to have for dinner. All the tension, all the emotion, remained where it had to on the golf course. Inside.

He turned to Cubby before speaking in a firm, decisive voice. "Nine-iron."

He took his stance. He checked his target one last time. How to calm his nerves at this moment?

Be enough!

Faxon watched his ball fly toward the pond. The shot had felt a little fat—hitting the ball high on the clubface, the result of swinging with too steep an arc.

But the ball came to rest on the green, just fifteen feet from the hole. Faxon's relief was palpable, but he still had to putt.

Pleasant Valley, like most golf courses, was designed with a combination of par-three, -four, and -five holes that added up to seventy-two strokes for a round of eighteen. The figure harks back to the layout of Royal St. Andrews in Scotland, where over time the course became eighteen holes (there was just enough land for that number). However, eighteen-hole courses sometimes have a par of less than seventy-two strokes, and, very occasionally, more. Typically, a par-72 course has four par threes, four par fives, and twelve par fours. In setting par for a hole, several factors are involved, but the critical one is usually distance (though, with the technology in clubmaking and ball manufacture and advances in player fitness, distance has become a relative, even outmoded concept).

On a well-designed par four, such as the Pleasant Valley seventeenth, the combination of distance and difficulty requires a player of Brad Faxon's caliber to take two shots to reach the green. Getting onto the green in golf is called getting up; getting the ball in the hole is called getting down. With the two putts that all players are assumed to need to get down on any hole, the player who gets to the green in regulation and makes his putts will record four, the player who needs only one putt gets a birdie three, and the player who needs three will record bogey. Of course, some players take only one putt, regardless of how many strokes they need before putting, and some put their approach shots in the cup. Thus, a player can still birdie a par four with a bad approach shot followed by a great one.

Ben Hogan, one of the greatest golfers of all time, once suggested that putts count only half a stroke. His retirement from the game was hastened by the fear he felt standing over a short putt, and he argued that such a shot should not count the same as one of the famous five-irons he could hit 185 yards to a target just a few feet wide.

Paradoxically, a child has the physical strength necessary to make most putts. A child might have made Brad Faxon's putt on the seventeenth at Pleasant Valley. But of course a child would not have known what the putt meant.

Brad's father did. Careful to avoid making a remark within his son's earshot that could jar Brad's concentration, he said to several employees of his Fall River power company, "If Brad makes this, everyone has tomorrow off!"

As soon as he reached the green, Faxon studied the small space between his ball and the hole.

Three spike marks in the line.

There was nothing he could do about that. On the final day of a tournament you only putted greens without spike marks if you were in one of the early groups, far behind the leaders in your score. Brad was in the last pairing.

Cubby held the flagstick. As soon as the ball was on its way, he would remove it, or Brad would incur a two-stroke penalty if the ball hit the stick (and Cubby would be in trouble with his employer).

Silence.

Checking his line one more time, Faxon took his putter back, moving only his shoulders, then he brought it forward, the rest of his body outwardly still but his insides, he would later say, "juiced."

The ball started rolling toward the hole.

Cubby pulled the flagstick.

The ball looked like it was going to the right.

Then it caught the right edge of the cup.

A power lip-out? That was Faxon's phrase for a putt that accelerated away from the cup after kissing an edge.

But this ball fell, into the cup. And as it did, Faxon fell too, fell to the moist, green ground, where he lay motionless for several seconds, trying to comprehend what he had just done. Around him sustained cheering erupted, while he remained still and supine.

It was going to the right. Never looked like it was going in.

I've won.

Still got to play eighteen.

THE WEEK AFTER he won the tournament at Pleasant Valley, Faxon competed at that year's Greater Hartford Open. During the pro-am a friend carried his bag for a few holes.

"Just don't line up any putts for me," Faxon joked.

Trying to stay on a roll that would continue through the rest of the summer, he gave some unsolicited advice to one of his amateur playing partners of that day.

"You've got a sound swing," Brad encouraged him. "But you do something I have a tendency to do myself sometimes," he added kindly. "Once you're set, once you've picked your target and taken your stance, don't wait. Swing!"

He was delighted to be greeted by a golfing fan at that tournament with a quizzical "Who are you?"

"I'm Brad Faxon," he smiled, signing an autograph for the fan.

"Yeah? You ever done something, you know, won any tournaments or anything?"

"Hey, Cubby," he said as they strolled down the next fairway. "You won't believe this guy I just met." And the two of them laughed.

"Stay outside the ropes," Cubby once warned an interloper at a tournament.

"But Cubby," the man protested, "I have an armband." Actually, in that case, a red ribbon and black button, on his left arm, the PGA Tour's equivalent of a golf pass for lucky members of that semi-pampered group, the media.

"I don't care what you have on your arm. We had a guy following us around a few weeks ago with one of those and he was getting in the way. I don't want *anyone* getting in Fax's way here."

During a pro-am round when the rope rule wasn't in effect, Cubby quietly exploded after an idle question hit another caddy nerve.

From the tee of the fifteenth at the TPC at River Highlands, an old nursery turned into a twice-rebuilt course with high-priced, empty house lots lining its chemically bombarded fairways and slime-colored ponds, the approach to the tantalizingly close green seemed benign. Even a good amateur player would be tempted to drive the short hole, with such a wide expanse of well-mowed fringe in front. Surely a pro would have no difficulty in making a decision about what club to use.

"Why's he hesitating?" someone asked.

Cubby's cold stare only heightened curiosity. After Faxon finally chose to hit a driver, which came up short, Cubby handed Brad his putter. Then with his head he motioned to his questioner to follow him, off to the side of the fairway.

"There's a lake up ahead, past the green. See?"

Of course. Anyone could see it from the tee, though it was

hard to realize how close its edge came to the back side of the green.

"You pull your driver, you're wet," Cubby continued.

That explained Faxon's momentary hesitation in club selection. But Cubby wasn't finished.

"Listen very carefully. When a person asks a question like you just did, if Fax had heard that, it might have put an idea in his head. A bad idea. Don't ever ask a question like that again when he's playing, never."

Cubby and Fax would have clashed regularly were it not for a shared sense of humor, bordering on the absurd. A fan at a pro-am event once mistook Cubby for Red Sox pitcher Frank Viola. To encourage the confusion, Brad immediately started calling Cubby by the name Frank.

Once during a rain delay, Cubby left the course with Faxon's clubs as soon as the siren sounded. Under the rules, Faxon could still finish the hole he was on—if he had his clubs. Many other players would get angry over such an incident, but Faxon laughed instead.

"I elected to putt," said Faxon afterward. "But my caddy elected to go in the clubhouse."

The episode was reminiscent in spirit of the last round of the 1991 Canadian Open, in which Faxon was too far behind in the final round to finish well. So he and Cubby devised a stratagem to make the last holes interesting. After each drive, Cubby would estimate with precision the distance Faxon had to the green. For a pro, the difference of just a few yards is critical in his selection of clubs. In Canada that day, Faxon calculated his correct club and then purposely played the wrong one, to force himself to be creative in his approach. He ended up shooting a low score anyway, five strokes better than his befuddled playing partner, Jay Don Blake.

"What does that prove?" he was later asked.

"That sometimes it doesn't matter!" he replied. In fact what he had done was an unusual athletic feat, utilizing the same skill that enabled him to avoid carrying a third wedge like most of his fellow pros. Faxon was so clever with his pitching and sand wedges that he could pop a ball into the air at almost any angle without changing clubs and still make it come to rest approximately where he wanted it to. Having fun during a practice round earlier in the Pleasant Valley tournament week, he had put on an exhibition of such greenside shotmaking for the other players in his group.

"I wouldn't try that in a round even if I knew how to do it," said former touring pro Dana Quigley, for whom Faxon used to caddy as a boy, and whom he had soundly beaten in the 1983 Q-School. Quigley was now a club pro, but he still played via special exemption or local qualifying in a few tour events. He was astonished at his former caddy's prowess and artistry with his wedge.

"Goddam."

SHARKBITE

AS FAR AS practicing on the range, all that does is hone your swing. If you're working on something, that's where you hone it. When you get out on the golf course, you play a totally different type of golf than what you do on the range. You see the target, you see the shot you want to hit, and you've got to play it. Now, on the range, you're practicing that shot after shot, and then even if you are practicing it, when you get out on the golf course and if you're practicing a one-hundred-and-fifty-four-yard eight-iron, that one hundred and fifty-four yards might be uphill or downhill, so it's a seven- or nine-iron. So all the range does for you is just hone your skill and hone your muscles, so when you get under pressure your body just executes what you've practiced.

I DON'T PERSONALLY think about my swing when I'm actually competing. All I do is think about the shot at hand and trust my swing. You don't have time to think about it out there.

The average touring professional who's made it is a feel player, as opposed to the fellow who seems to have all the mechanics but for some illusive reason doesn't seem able to stick. A feel player can make adjustments on the golf course. I've made adjustments on the golf course many times when my swing is not right. I can go from the driving range knowing that I'm going to have a day where I've really got to be careful because my swing's not right, and so I make adjustments, play the golf course by feel. I've done that many times, but I haven't thought about my golf swing out there, because I'm trying to figure out the best way to get from point A to point B without hurting myself. You've got to have a thought in your mind each day about how you're going to approach your swing of that day.

Rhythm?

Ball position?

You don't actually think about the swing. I don't, anyway.

I LOVE THE COMPETITIVE side of the game. I love it when your juices are flowing, when you've got to hit that five-iron into the eighteenth hole. Everybody might say to me why didn't I just lay it up short of the green and get it on, and I say, "Well, what happens if my opponent holes the shot? Then I look like some guy who's made the wrong decision." Then you're just playing somebody else's game and not playing your own.

NO FEAR

"IT'S BASICALLY AN easy game, made hard by us because it is a slow process and you become afraid," according to BBC television commentator and former Ryder Cup player Peter Allis. "Only the very best can control that fear."

Very few like to admit it.

"Looking over my career, I'd say two words characterize my playing style," Greg Norman has boasted. Despite the large evidence to the contrary, he says those two words are "No fear." His remarks are reminiscent of Tom Watson's almost a decade earlier: "The most effective way to deal with stress is to do something well."

Nearly ninety years ago, in a slim volume entitled *The Mystery of Golf*, a writer and amateur golfer named Arnold Haultain sought to assuage this fear by answering the question "In what does the secret of golf lie?"

"Not in one thing, but in many," he answered. "And in many so mysteriously conjoined, so incomprehensibly interwoven, as to baffle analysis. The mind plays as large a part as the muscles; and perhaps the moral nature as large a part as the mind— though this would carry us into regions deeper even than these depths of psychology. Suffice it to say that all golfers know that golf must be played seriously, earnestly; as seriously, as earnestly, as life."

One evening at a U.S. Open a few years ago, after most of the contestants in the first round had finished playing, the last trio of competitors were making their approach shots on fourteen, their obscurity so great that even the roving marshal who accompanied them didn't know one of their names. Their galleries were nonexistent.

In the growing darkness of a summer's night, departing fans crossed the fourteenth fairway when it was cleared of the final golfers and continued across the contiguous thirteenth, where Tom Watson had had an awful four-putt that day. From a knoll there on the thirteenth his wife, Linda, who followed him around the course, had grimaced as she looked at the slick green during those putts. The green was empty in the evening, and quiet. Quiet, too, was the twelfth, on the way to the fairways of an adjacent nine-hole course being used that week as a parking lot. An unused green on that course was roped off. Someone had found a range ball nearby and thrown it onto the stubby surface.

Curtis Strange won that Open, the first of two consecutive U.S. Opens he captured (the second of which turned out to be his last tournament victory in the United States during a period that extended over six years through 1995). Greg Norman, after injuring a wrist when his clubhead struck a rock during a third-round swing, had to withdraw. Brad Faxon missed the cut. Many of the other contestants that year would soon play themselves out of professional golf, at least at the tour level. A then promising player named Rick Dalpos, for example, who in 1988 was competing in his second U.S. Open, by 1995 was not even an exempt player on golf's Nike Tour, an official minor-league circuit started by the PGA Tour in 1990.

While Greg Norman may never worry about playing on the Nike Tour, and Brad Faxon, despite some lean years in the 1980s, may seem a sure thing after his successes in the first half of the 1990s, there is really no security for anyone who plays professional golf. Fine players have lost what they all call "it." Nick Faldo's childhood rival Sandy Lyle, who was Masters champion the year of Strange's first U.S. Open title, in 1990 plummeted to 175th place in tour earnings.

YET ANOTHER ECHELON of players competes on minor circuits. The Hooters-Jordan tour is an eight-month-long odyssey to such golf meccas as Rantoul, Illinois. Players who haven't been able to qualify for the Nike Tour may also be found competing in regional professional events. Pete Morgan of Cape Cod, Massachusetts, played the New England circuit in 1994 and, after winning the Massachusetts Open, received an invitation to play in the New England Classic, where he missed the cut. The following fall he qualified for the Nike Tour, but his standing did not get him into every tournament. He did not make a cut until July, when he earned $900 in Buffalo.

A short, lean golfer with close-cropped blond hair, Morgan grew up in a golfing family. His brother, Jay, a businessman, was club champion at his home course. Peter visited him at least once a summer, and the brothers would play together at Jay's course, in a foursome with Jay's two young children. Pete's appearance usually caused a small stir at the club. The father of the club pro might follow him for a few holes, marveling at the man's distance off the tee and hoping he'd start making a few putts.

"If he'd only make a few more putts": invariably, that is the refrain that accompanies discussion of any good golfer having problems, whether it be Tom Watson or Pete Morgan. A few putts. If Pete Morgan made a few more putts, he would be playing regularly on the Nike Tour. For Tom Watson, the difference meant winning a tournament again.

For Greg Norman, a few more putts would have meant at least half a dozen major championships and ten or more regular tour victories.

T.C. SHOOK HIS head when someone asked too many questions. But all the way along Route A1A from Jacksonville Beach to Ponte Vedra, Florida, a distance of approximately ten miles, T.C. talked about golf.

T.C. drove the shuttle the hotel provided for members of the media who were attending the Players Championship, since the PGA Tour had designated the Jacksonville Beach Comfort Inn (Oceanfront) as media headquarters. But most members of the media appeared to be staying elsewhere, the Sawgrass Marriott if they were able to get a room there and could afford it, and just about everyone had rented a car.

More than ten years since his attempts to play the PGA Tour, T.C. worked now as a greeter and glorified gofer for the Jacksonville Beach Comfort Inn (Oceanfront), a functional concrete affair on the water with a bar and a pool, patio views from many of the rooms, cable television, Touch-tone phones, and a breakfast buffet that included store-bought doughnuts. T.C. welcomed guests at the inn and made golfing arrangements for them, getting them on nearby resort courses or giving them directions to the nearest public layout, the Jacksonville Beach Golf Club. If he was free he'd even give them a ride over. But this week he'd been giving people rides to another course, the TPC at Sawgrass.

No telling for sure, but if things had gone a little differently for T.C. back in his own playing days he might have been competing in this very tournament instead of giving people rides to it. But T.C. was not a man to complain; nor, for that matter, to provide very specific information about his brief stint as one of golf's finest, a career so obscure that there is no record of it at PGA Tour headquarters, where organization and computerization of player statistics did not begin in earnest until the 1980s. Rather than talk about himself, T.C. mentioned his buddy Mike Smith, a journeyman pro from Alabama who *was* playing in 1993, even if he practically had to *buy* his own golf shoes while some of the younger guys got *paid* to wear them. Didn't Rocco Mediate have a deal with Foot-Joy?

"But you watch," said T.C.. "Soon's one of those guys starts playing a little bad, they drop him. Just like that."

For every Rocco Mediate in pro golf there are fifteen or twenty Mike Smiths; for every player of Mike Smith's caliber, there are probably hundreds who play as well but for one reason or another haven't made it (and there are also some lesser talents whose fortitude enables them to defy the odds). For each would-be there are literally thousands of golfers, some of whom hold jobs as teaching professionals at golf courses, who on a given day can shoot a good score but realistically have no chance of competing on tour. American men's professional golf, the world's premier tour in terms of purses, course conditions, and the level of competition, represents the very small top of a very large pyramid, with a reward structure skewed toward the elite. As a pastime, golf may be becoming more democratic, but as a profession it remains a meritocracy. Though the top 125 players each year retain their playing privileges for the next season, even many of them have to struggle to make ends meet.

"PRO GOLF SUCKS!"

By any other measure of success than the golf tour's yardstick of the top 125 money winners, Patrick Burke was a success. Born in Florida in 1962 and now a resident of a Los Angeles suburb, Burke had once finished tied for sixth in a PGA Tour event, the 1992 Bellsouth Classic, played in Atlanta, Georgia. The bearded, diminutive former amateur hockey player earned a check there for $34,750, the highest in his career; among the players he finished ahead of that week was the previous year's British Open winner, Ian Baker-Finch (whose swing problems were beginning to lead him into a long, shocking slide to mediocrity). But a year later he was having trouble with his whole game.

"My driving sucks, my irons suck, my short game sucks, my health sucks," Burke sneered at himself. "My head sucks." If things did not improve, he, too, might soon be looking for other work.

Perhaps in response to the terror it provokes, golf is supposed to reveal character as does no other sport. Tom Watson once became embroiled in a nasty rules discussion that also revealed the prickliness behind his calm exterior. He accused Gary Player, another golfing eminence, of cheating during a televised Skins game in Arizona, no less. Watson charged Player with moving something that was rooted in the ground, in order to improve his lie. This was a clear violation of the rules, but Player denied the accusation. Nevertheless, Player's clean-cut image was tarnished, while Watson's hard-nosed reputation was reinforced. The two men have rarely spoken since, and Player went out of his way once to suggest that Watson's 1982 U.S. Open title was tainted by Watson's use of allegedly illegal irons.

MONEY IS THE measure of a professional golfer's achievement. There is no other yardstick, comparable to a baseball player's batting average, that reflects the cumulative performance of a professional golfer, though tour statisticians have tried to create one. The only box score that matters on the PGA Tour is written with a dollar sign.

Even the language of professional golf is partly pecuniary, from the weekly top money rankings published in newspapers to the meager earnings, reported in the tour's own newsletter, of players whose small failures may mean financial disaster. If you tune in a televised tournament you will hear an announcer say somberly, "This putt could be worth forty thousand dollars." With the evolution of the Senior PGA Tour from two tournaments in 1980 to forty a year, with total purses rising in that period from $250,000 to an amount enabling the top players to compete in earnings with their counterparts on the regular tour, there has been a similar emphasis on money. And that affects the way the competitors approach their work. Don January, a crusty veteran of the Senior Tour, when approached for an interview immediately asked, "How much?" Upon being told nothing, his response was, "Nice try."

Though the players are independent contractors, they are part of a carefully presented "product" whose overall annual revenues exceed $200 million. Because a portion of that money is donated to charity, with the remainder used to fund administrative expense, the PGA Tour is legally a nonprofit corporation; prize money for tournaments it does not directly run is presented by tournament sponsors, and those tournaments also donate to designated charities.

Underlying the neurotic personality of the tour product are many rules, some codified (no shorts or blue jeans) and others not (no boasting), in order that the public see only a protected image of the athletes. It often seems that every pro is every other pro's best friend as a matter of tour policy, and no one broaches a difference. As a matter of human nature, of course, these men cannot always stay on good terms with one another. In the tour's self-described family, as in any other, a certain tension enters the picture. Now and then.

The key component of the image the tour projects so successfully is the marquee personalities, Greg Norman and the mysterious Fred "Boom Boom" Couples (whose apparent effortlessness belies his golfing prowess as 1991 and 1992 Player of the Year and past Masters champion) and Nick Price, or the Englishman who for several years didn't even compete as a regular member of the tour but still managed to win more money than many of the men who do, Nick Faldo. When one of those men has his game together, he seems to take the difficulty out of golf. But that also adds to the mysteriousness of it, because it is so hard to understand why things click when they do.

THE AMERICAN PROFESSIONAL golf tour is a television program, with the media people who write about it and announce it serving as part of the program while they move around the country with the tour. To attend one of those tournaments in person, then, is to be part of the studio audience that views the filming or videotaping of a television program, but the scenes offstage, away from the course, aren't usually filmed.

The night was filled with the sound of tree frogs or cicadas. Past the empty parking lots in the service area of the Tournament Players Club some men were drinking beer in a trailer that had been set up for marshals, who were all volunteers, even the ones who got parking-lot duty and never saw any golf while they were volunteering. They got to drink beer afterward in the trailer.

A reporter told the man in charge he had missed his shuttle.

"What hotel you staying at? Let me call them for you. Want a beer?"

The reporter said no, then changed his mind.

He had almost finished the Michelob when Adam arrived. T.C.'s replacement today, Adam was a former surfer whose wife, Amy, was one of the hotel's reservation managers. Adam was a carpenter, but he'd been laid off. Working the shuttle shift at the Comfort Inn this weekend brought in a little extra income, and it gave Adam something to do. Judging by his cough, he shouldn't have been doing anything; he'd picked up a bad cold recently. But he wasn't going to spend the weekend in bed.

Everyone else he was driving was already back at the hotel. He could have gone home but instead had waited for the reporter because he had promised he would.

"How you doing today, man?" asked Adam.

Since they had met the day before, that was the way he addressed him. Adam was polite. He never made another person feel he was in a hurry.

"Who'd you see?" Adam asked.

The reporter had taken the other front seat. "Okay if I drink this in here?" he said, moving the hand that held the remains of his beer. And then, in response to his question, "Faxon mostly."

"How'd he play?"

"Not very well. The round just went badly. After he had that sixty-seven on Thursday, too."

"That's golf."

"Yeah. When he was done Brad looked at his wife, Bonnie, who walked most of the round with him, and said, 'I don't know what to do. Hit balls? Go to the clubhouse?' "

"And what did she say?"

"She said, 'You could give me a kiss.' "

"That was it?"

They had left the lot and driven past one of the many sentries on duty during the tournament who were guarding the real estate adjacent to the course, huge, expensive homes built on the former site of a giant swamp. Two brothers, Jerome and Paul Fletcher, had owned the land, and they sold the first big chunk for $1. No one could understand why they had done that, but after the course was built, and the first homes, and then more homes, and more courses, after that development cycle was set in motion, there was a tremendous demand for more land. And the brothers still owned that land. This time they didn't sell for $1.

"Then he did go hit balls," the reporter answered Adam. He could see the scene in his head, the sun low in the horizon, the range darkening. Brad had stopped to chat with another pro, a fellow named Dillard Pruitt who had grown up and still lived in Greenville, South Carolina, site of Faxon's alma mater, Furman University. The same age as Faxon, Pruitt had not made it onto the tour until 1988. Since then he had had modest success, posting one victory, in 1991.

"Hey, Fax."

"Hey, Dillard."

And then Faxon had grabbed a metal basket of balls and walked along the range to an open spot, spilling the balls before his caddy, John, who was substituting for Cubby because Cubby was back in Sun Valley.

"I'm gonna hit balls for five minutes," Fax had said. And he hit balls for fifteen.

"Watch me, John. Over the top on that one? Squared?

"Okay, I'm aiming for that yellow flag.

"Now *that* yellow flag.

"Now those three white flags."

A friend of Faxon's, a former pro football player named Ernest, had appeared.

Ernest knew Brad well enough to have greeted Bonnie Faxon with a hug on the range.

Brad reached into his golf bag and retrieved the pouch with the tie string in which all the pros seem to carry their watches and wallets while they are playing.

"All right, Ernest. Here's a Ben Franklin that says you can't hit that yellow flag out there."

THERE WERE A number of courses in the area that hotel guests played, but unlike the others the Jacksonville Beach Golf Club required no advanced arrangements to get on. It was a public municipal course, a "muni." Its chief advantage to guests was its low greens fee and proximity to the hotel, which meant if he was lucky a guest today might get in eighteen holes before the final round of the Players Championship.

The drive was no more than ten minutes. Entering the parking lot for the course an out-of-town golfer passed the driving range, already crowded. But the area around the first tee was fairly quiet. The golfer walked to a bench, where he changed into the golf shoes he had packed. The golfer put his sneakers in the bag, then stepped into the pro shop, a bare room in a bare building.

"That will be twenty-five dollars and fifty-one cents."

The golfer walked back outside, found his cart and the assigned playing partner who would share it with him, and practiced a few putts. There was an old seven-iron in the bag someone had lent him, and he tried a few chips with it. The balls he was using were new Titleists he had found at the tournament yesterday. They had been hit by the pros beyond the fence by the bushes that bordered the far end of the driving range. They looked exactly like the Titleists so many of the pros played, except the word "Practice" had been stamped on each one of them.

Several months had passed since the man's last round of golf back home. He had not come over this morning to shoot a score. He just wanted to try doing what he had been watching others do all week.

He used an old borrowed driver on the first hole and topped his shot, but it landed in the fairway. With his three-iron he hit his next one well, the ball landing just in front of the green. Perhaps all that golf reading he had been doing during the winter was going to pay a dividend here. Because the ground in front of the green looked soft, he hit a nine-iron instead of the seven, trying to loft the ball and land it just on the green, near the flagstick.

He missed the green. In fact, he almost missed hitting the ball, advancing it only a few yards, his nine-iron clipping the scrub grass behind the ball and then gouging the ground underneath, as if he were trying to hit out of a sand bunker.

"Don't worry about it," said his cart partner, a Jacksonville schoolteacher who was skipping his usual visit at the Ponte Vedra Beach Club to play this Sunday-morning eighteen. He was going to the tournament, too, he said, but not until later. He was a marshal, but they didn't need him early because he was working one of the last holes and no one would be playing it until nearly noon.

The man's partner and he now moved on to the second hole, with out of bounds on the left and a pond on the right. The man hadn't paid attention to the pond before he teed up his ball. Only after his swing did he notice how large it was. As his ball flew off the clubface and he watched helplessly, the pond seemed to grow bigger and bigger, just as it did on the famous seventeenth hole at the TPC, a par three where the green was completely surrounded by water. Splash!

THE LOCAL NEWSCASTS on the television were featuring Players Championship coverage, with a shot of a smiling Nick Price holding overhead the glass trophy he had won, along with a check for $450,000 and a ten-year exemption to play in tour events. It was the then thirty-six-year-old's sixth tour win, and fifth since 1991, his first having come ten years earlier. His winning score was 270, eighteen under par and five shots ahead of Bernhard Langer, who had snuck into second when Greg Norman mishit a seven-iron at the pin on the seventeenth and the ball drifted right and landed in the water.

The announcer's voice reminded the viewer of a man he had met coming down here on the plane. He had been seated next to this man, who was making his first flight. The man drank beer the whole way and talked incessantly, even after the viewer feigned a nap instead of eating lunch.

When, the man kept asking him, when did he think they would arrive?

"When the plane lands," he had answered. The man thought he was being sarcastic. Actually, he was sharing with him a small prayer.

Smoothly, the plane had climbed to its cruising altitude, but he had a terrible feeling in his gut, a feeling that he could remember now, the kind of premonition he associated with disaster. So far as he aware, he had never been close to being in a crash. But as he watched the replay of the Shark's tee shot on seventeen he was certain he knew the feeling, the powerless inability to control one's destiny. Though he had witnessed the Shark's errant tee shot in person, it seemed somehow more definitive now that he had watched it again on the television screen.

GREG HAD STARTED that day at minus eleven with a greeting from Paul Azinger. "Play good, Greg," Paul said. And he had. A good out from a waste bunker on one. A great putt on two that just missed birdie. A twenty-five-footer for birdie on seven to go twelve under. He could see Price on the hole behind him. Nick was at fifteen under then, three ahead of the Shark. And

Nick was not folding. It was some time since Nick had realized, "I can play with these guys." He wasn't going to crack today.

But would Greg catch him?

A bogey at nine didn't help, nor did the way the bogey occurred. Greg was just about to hit his drive on the same par five where the day before Brad Faxon had lost a ball in a tree when a fan's beeper went off.

"Take your time, Greg," Tony Navaro said.

"What for?" said another fan as he watched the Shark launch another three-hundred-yard shot.

But something was out of sync. After laying up with his second, the Shark put his third in a bunker and couldn't get it up and down.

But he did two holes later, on the par-five eleventh. Back to twelve under, which is where he stayed until birdies at fifteen and sixteen.

"I'd pay good dollars to see this," said one of the photographers who was following his group. Greg's second shot right at the flag on sixteen had just stopped two inches from the water.

SOON THE TELEVISION screen was filled with the image of more golfers, this time seniors. The New Zealand lefthander Bob Charles had won this week's event, the Doug Sanders Celebrity Classic. Charles's check of $75,000 was little more than the $67,500 Tom Watson had won for finishing tenth at the TPC.

But the golf, the viewer reflected as he stepped outside onto his first-floor balcony—Oceanfront!—had been no easier. He peered over the railing at the empty kidney-shaped swimming pool. He thought he could hear voices coming from the Jacuzzi at the end of the pool by the bar. A swimmer there reminded him of a woman he had seen that day at the course, wearing tight pants and white socks with the cuffs turned down. This fashion statement was a common sight in tour galleries.

Equally common was the lady he had overheard on the second hole in the huge group following the Shark. After a bogey today at the first, where his drive had landed in a waste bunker on the right—the same waste bunker where Davis Love had hit several shots when he was telling those children at the clinic about making the same swing—Greg was eleven under for the tournament. It was hot, sunny, and windy, and the Shark seemed a little off his game. His approach shot on two went way right, and the subsequent chip was strong. He seemed oblivious to the throng around him, including the woman, who exclaimed to her husband as Norman strode by, "He's gorgeous, like Crocodile Dundee. That's an awesome hat he's wearing."

Because of his blond hair and his boast, at an interview following his first Masters, in 1981, that he had fished for sharks in his native Australia, Norman had been given his nickname. But over the course of his career it had sometimes seemed a burden to live up to. Rather than being a mask that protected him, the image of the Shark could cheapen Norman's human response to the game's fate. On the course, the Shark could seem nothing more than an icon.

THE NIGHT BEFORE, in the nearly empty parking lot by the TPC clubhouse, Brad Faxon stood before the open trunk of his Buick, his clubs to one side of the car. It was Saturday evening, with the final round of the 1993 Players Championship still to come, but he was headed home to Orlando.

An Orlando neighbor was helping Faxon with his gear, which he had to move from the Buick. Out of the tournament because of an illegal drop he had taken on the eighteenth hole of the third round, he had to turn in his courtesy car. He had already traded in his tournament outfit for blue jeans.

The clubhouse door opened and out walked Greg Norman, who spotted Faxon in the parking lot. Norman had shot 68 on Saturday and was in good position to take a run at Nick Price, the leader since the first day of the tournament. Before leaving the clubhouse the Shark had apparently learned of Faxon's infraction, which had not been caught by the rules officials until after Faxon's round was over.

Instead of playing his third shot on the eighteenth after moving some television cables that were in his way, Brad had taken a drop. Afterward, talking to a tour official before lunch, Faxon had mentioned what happened. His entire round had been difficult, with the front nine including a triple bogey and a ball lost in a tree. So an inadvertent illegal drop at the eighteenth had been a kind of final straw. But Faxon hadn't let it bother him. He had been angry after the triple, and confounded after the lost ball, but he had played himself out of the tournament by the time he reached the eighteenth. The small check he might have won with a completed tournament on Sunday would not have made a big impact on his finances.

THE QUESTION YOU frequently hear on any course where the pros play is "Anybody done anything?" When you see a score go up indicating that a player has just birdied or eagled a hole, you say, "He must have done something."

When Tom Watson, in the third round of the 1993 Players Championship, hit an errant drive on the twelfth and then had to punch out from an impossible lie by an oak tree, his third shot finished three feet from the hole. He had done something.

Then Tom missed the three-foot putt.

Now he had really done something.

So had Brad Faxon in the same round. Still at two under on six, he hit his approach behind a tree.

"I'll bounce it off," he said. But the shot came up short. Then he almost chipped in for par—almost did something.

Bogey. One under.

Now the disastrous seventh. Pushed drive that lands by a tree. Hits a tree coming out and is now behind another tree. Hits a branch coming out. "Oh, no!" Into the water. Takes a drop and now lies four. Gets to the green and two-putts for triple bogey.

Brad had done something.

He scowled. Walking to the eighth tee, he was silent. No greetings to friends or family. Still to come was the lost ball on nine and the DQ after the ruling on eighteen. By then he had found his sense of humor again.

Hit the road, Brad.

"HEY, BRAD," GREG smiled, stopping by the car. For once, no fans had gathered and Greg could just be himself.

"Fuck you!" Greg said with great good humor. Then he laughed, obviously referring to Faxon's disqualification. Faxon looked up and smiled back.

Then the Shark was gone, into the Florida night, just as he had left this day, Sunday, after his bid to catch Nick Price had failed. Long before Price had exited the eighteenth-green trophy presentation and appeared at a press conference, where he bought champagne for the media, Greg Norman had changed out of his golf shoes and slipped through the back door of the clubhouse, where Muzak was still playing in the Gallery of Champions (*Here on display within this Tournament Players Club you see the symbols of triumph presented to PGA Tour champions, those whose talent and distinction have earned them a place in this Gallery of Champions. Welcome*), the trophy cases set next to tables with fresh cut flowers. Now, holding the hand of daughter Morgan-Leigh, signing autographs all the way to his car, Greg drove away from the TPC, and just like T.C. earlier in the week, even the Great White Shark got caught in traffic.

TEACHING PRO TOM Toski likes to say, "Golf is an intelligent game played by intelligent people stupidly." Toski is a member of an illustrious golfing family. His brother Bob was a successful touring pro in the 1950s and a member of the Senior Tour in the 1980s.

"You've got a twelve-ounce club and a two-ounce ball, and it takes nothing to hit it," Toski continues.

"But most people want to start off hitting the ball two hundred and fifty yards, when they should be at home, practicing their chip shots. That's what my brothers and I used to do when we couldn't afford to play on a real course. That's how you get the feel of the club.

"I always tell my students, 'Never force the feel. Feel the force.' You've got to let things happen."

It was advice any beginner could forget, just like the touring pros at the Players Championship, the Shark and his younger competitor and friend Brad Faxon, and the other men—146 of them, at the start—who had been playing this tantalizingly difficult game for money in Ponte Vedra this week. Everyone playing golf there knew the fear a pro felt on the first tee, knew the sadness when a great round died because of a stupid mistake or carelessness or bad luck.

Knew the way the wind sounded in the trees on the range while he warmed up, maybe even how it sounded as he was waking up at the Jacksonville Beach Comfort Inn, which might have reminded him of something in his life—a lover, a father, a friend. All that went into a pro's game each day, went in with the conversation over breakfast with that cute waitress in the hotel and the grizzled look on the face of the fellow at the bag room whom he talked to about the day's weather prediction when he picked up his bag (because his caddy wasn't allowed into the locker room). When he asked the man matter-of-factly how he was, the reply stunned him momentarily out of his competitive shell.

"Wife's got cancer, don't know how long she has."

The smell of shoe polish in the locker room and the sight of shaving cream and shampoo on the marble sink, the smell of cigarette smoke in the bathroom and ashes on the floor of the toilet stall from the last guy that was in there, and the mist over those palm trees by the practice green mixed with his memory of the flight he took last week and those legs he saw in the seat across the aisle as the plane was landing and he was waking from his nap. Now another match, every day another round.

"Wonder whether *it* will be there, wonder if that little stance change will make a difference, wonder what my kids are doing this morning."

How did he make sense of that awful story about the robbery in the newspaper this morning?

Jeez, there were convenience places like that everywhere he traveled, everywhere he played.

What was he doing playing golf in a world where that happened?

What else should he do?

"Got to support my family. These are my priorities. God. My family. Golf."

Could he keep it straight on the first? Will he remember to hold his finish?

"Just get it out there and get my par and be patient."

No problem.

SHARKBITE

WHATEVER ONE DOES in the past reflects in how they perform in the future. People draw off negatives in life and they draw off positives. If you've had a whole bunch of negatives in your life and you haven't had a lot of positives, then you're going to feel, how come all this stuff is happening to me? In any walk of life. If you draw off a lot of positives in life—take golf, for example—if you win, and you know how to win, then you draw off that positive.

Golf is very much an individual sport. There's a physical aspect and there's a mental aspect. There's time away from family, time on the road, home with the family. There's so many different permutations, combinations, within the game of golf that no other athlete ever experiences, because even in tennis you've got an opponent to hit the ball back to you. You're the individual swinging the racket, but you have somebody who can make you look good or look bad. In a team sport, if you have a great offensive team and a poor defensive side, you're going to get beaten no matter how many points you rack up. The same with basketball. You can see the relationship there.

But in golf, you have to do it all yourself.

That's why the Jack Nicklauses of the world and the Raymond Floyds and the Lee Trevinos are so successful, because they go on and do what they like to do. They trust their innate ability and play the game the way they want to play it, not the way someone else is telling them to play.

TALKING TO A FADE

BETTER THAN MOST men, Paul Moran understands the high-stakes world of pro golf in which Greg Norman competes, even though during his active playing career he existed only at its periphery. The stakes were Paul Moran's life.

Whenever Moran tells this story, the small details vary slightly. But the anguish in his voice remains the same. The year was 1972 and Moran was playing in the Phoenix Open, a tournament on the professional golf tour. It was the final round, and, with only a few holes to go, Moran was tied with the eventual winner. Such a victory, the first in his career, could have changed his life.

"We came to a par three," Moran recalls, and he begins to get a faraway look in his eyes. He vividly remembers what happened in Phoenix many years ago. The torment of the memory is palpable.

"There was water in front of the green. I played a long iron shot, but I was short. Hit it into the water."

Moran couldn't believe what he had done. How he wished he could have that one swing over! Crestfallen, he had to take a penalty stroke before putting another ball in play. His score on the par three was six, a triple. That one mistake left him with an eventual score of 276 and put him out of contention in the tournament, won by Homero Blancas in a playoff over Lanny Wadkins, who each finished the four rounds of regulation play at 273. Moran never came as close to winning on tour again.

A few years later, with his finances precarious and his game still struggling, the former Haverhill, Massachusetts, resident quit touring and took a full-time job as a golf teacher. An entire decade passed before Moran met Blancas and his other old colleagues on the golf course once more.

By then, Blancas had no memory of being chased by Moran at Phoenix in 1972. Instead, Blancas recollected the playoff, one of four victories that earned his reputation as one of the better players in his era. But Moran looked back wistfully at Phoenix and thought of what might have been.

Moran left the regular tour in 1978 with *total* career earnings of not quite $65,000, less than many pros in the 1990s pay their caddies per season. Then, while he spent the next ten years teaching at several New England courses, the senior tour developed into a financial bonanza for veteran pros. By 1988, when Moran turned fifty—the minimum age for eligibility as a Senior Tour player—total purses were almost $15 million and escalating (to an amount today more than double).

Moran knows that golf can be incredibly frustrating, and complete golfing success ever elusive. But he trusts his swing, which he continued to perfect while he was teaching. And he never forgot what one of his fellow pros called the "dry-throat" thrill of competition. With the Senior Tour, Moran realized a kind of salvation might be at hand. He could resume doing what he'd dreamed of since he caddied as a boy at the Haverhill Country Club: play tournament golf for a living.

The only way Moran could play regularly on the Senior Tour was to qualify. To do that, he had to play in two nerveracking qualifying tournaments and finish in the top eight. The odds were against him—several hundred other golfers were also trying. And the memory of his earlier failures, epitomized by that triple bogey at Phoenix in 1972, was difficult to erase. Unlike Greg Norman, who had also lost tournaments he thought he was going to win, Moran had never been in position to win again.

Moran wanted desperately to be among the men he considered his peers. He was encouraged by his showing in two tournaments that he entered via special, one-time-only qualification. He believed he belonged on the Senior Tour. He started taking better care of his health. He quit drinking coffee and cut down smoking cigarettes. He began riding a bicycle that his wife gave him.

In the qualifying finals, Moran just made it, with his seventh-place tie. But other barriers to Moran's senior success remained.

SITTING IN THE air-conditioned men's locker room of the Nashawtuc Country Club in Concord, Massachusetts, Moran carefully tied the laces to the golf shoes that had been shined for him the night before by a clubhouse attendant. The time was around noon on the Tuesday before the Digital Seniors Classic began. Tuesday was a practice day, and Moran was about to play a full practice round, but first he needed to locate his caddy.

In the five months he'd been playing on the senior tour, Moran had won just over $37,000—or more than half the amount he'd collected in his entire ten years on the regular tour. His best finish had been a tie for tenth place in mid-June at the Northville Long Island Classic. His best score was a 62 in a pro-am round preceding a tournament in Syracuse ("the best round of my life," he called it). Overall, he stood in forty-seventh place on the Senior Tour money list—not bad, but not nearly enough to keep him from having to qualify all over again in the fall. To avoid that fate, he had to either win a tournament or make enough money to be among the top players on the money list.

That wasn't going to be easy. Many of the men against whom

he was competing had earned so much money during their regular careers that they would continue to receive an exemption to play on the Senior Tour as long as they wanted to. The only pressure on those men was to look good; they had nothing to prove.

Moreover, according to the unfair rules devised for the conduct of an official Senior Tour tournament, all golfers are not treated equally. Those such as Paul Moran in the lower echelons consistently receive poor starting times for the first round of each three-round tournament. In addition, they are ineligible to play in several of the tournaments, which are invitational affairs. But the prize money from those invitational tournaments is still counted in the final standings; the seniors do not compete on a level playing field.

Many associated with the Senior Tour see nothing wrong with this. Naturally, the stars don't complain; the system benefits them. In fact, they seem to begrudge the participation of any extras in their party. During a "media day" appearance at Nashawtuc, three-time Digital Seniors Classic champion Chi Chi Rodriguez refused to talk about the subject. Later, before conducting a youth clinic at Boston's Franklin Park, the animated, usually affable Rodriguez, when asked about Moran and other, similar players, snapped: "I beat them thirty years ago; I beat them now." The comment is typical of successful players, whose monomaniacal focus on themselves is a key to golfing success.

But it is also true, which anyone watching Chi Chi hit his trick shots would have understood instantly. During one routine, he explained how you could save money by shagging your own golf balls. Then he demonstrated by hitting a ball with his pitching wedge and actually catching ("shagging") it, midair, with the blade of the wedge. On the golf course, Rodriguez was regularly capable of feats requiring similar skills. Once, in a team tournament in Oregon, he hit such a poor drive that the ball did not reach the beginning of the fairway. Instead of getting upset or acting embarrassed, Chi Chi laughed at himself and got on with the business of rescuing a hole headed straight for disaster: one shot out of the rough, one more from the fairway to the green, only to wind up with a heartbreaking, but still remarkable two-putt for bogey. This kind of thing happens all the time in professional golf. At Spyglass Hill, one of the courses that is part of the Pebble Beach National Pro-Am rotation, Brad Faxon had about a ten-foot opening to get out of trouble in trees following a wayward tee shot on the sixteenth. Most golfers would have chosen to punch out sideways to the fairway, but Faxon calculated the angle of trajectory to the tree opening, which was at about the height of a two-story house, and calmly hit an iron shot that went through the clearing in the trees and landed within pitching-wedge distance of the green.

Moran had played too much golf to let Chi Chi's snub bother him. He was aware of the sentiment, but he knew better than to respond in kind. As his fellow pro Dick McNeill commented, "It's unfair, but the game's unfair." McNeill, who never played on the regular tour, had earned enough money as a businessman to support himself in his quest to be a successful Senior Tour player. But he had to try each week to qualify for one of the four open spots that are reserved for nonexempt players. Having too much fun to complain, McNeill hoped eventually to get a year's exemption with a high finish like Moran's at the qualifying school. "Knocking the door down," he called this.

The caste system among the seniors extends even to caddies. The famous players have their own regular caddies, while most of the others, such as Moran, employ a local or one of the nomads who follow the Senior Tour. Lately, Moran was using the services of a middle-aged man who called himself Mobile, the name of his hometown in Alabama. Other Senior Tour caddies included a jazz musician who went by the name of Piano Man and a fellow in a ten-gallon hat who was known, naturally, as Cowboy.

After he'd finished putting on his golf shoes, Moran still couldn't find Mobile. Some players would have cursed, but Moran just shrugged. Life on the Senior Tour was still too new to him for such an occurrence to be upsetting. He walked to the door of the guarded clubhouse and carried his huge black-and-white bag himself to the nearby cart area. As a concession to their age, all the seniors are permitted to ride golf carts—though their caddies then have to walk.

The temperature outside was hot, the air muggy. The weather reminded Moran of Georgia, where he had recently moved. He'd lived in Georgia before—in the mid-1970s he won several state golfing titles there—and he spoke with a slight Georgian drawl, mixed idiosyncratically with his native Massachusetts diction.

Though he wasn't a star, Moran enjoyed small perks. Under the supervision of the caddy master, a schoolteacher on vacation, someone put Moran's bag on a cart. Lettering on the bag advertised a new resort in Florida, the state where Moran had lived while qualifying for the Senior Tour. Moran was almost apologetic that the resort wasn't a well-known spa. One suspected that it was owned by a friend, just as the car he'd been driving all week was on loan from a Volvo dealer he grew up with and the house where he'd been staying was the home of one of his former golf pupils, a securities executive from nearby Lincoln.

Most of the paying public that day had come to see a nine-hole exhibition involving ten players in a format called a shootout. The participants earned extra money for this, but in another instance of the rich getting richer they were chosen primarily because they had already earned more money than others. So Moran was not in the shootout field. Instead, while he hit balls on the practice range, he got up a foursome with Dick McNeill, former touring pro Ken Still, and his old friend and opponent in the Phoenix Open Homero Blancas. With Mobile, who had miraculously appeared, they teed off at the tenth hole, since the shootout would be using the front nine. Still immediately began telling bad jokes.

"So this woman goes to see her physician and she says, 'Doctor, I have a personal question. Is it possible to conceive with anal sex?' And the doctor says, 'Of course it is. How do you think lawyers are born?' "

Many of the trees at Nashawtuc, an early-1960s layout, hadn't grown to their full height. So the golfers could often see their fellow competitors on adjacent fairways. One player was all by himself, patiently hitting as many as half a dozen balls from the spot where his drive had landed. A roar from the gallery watching the shootout erupted from afar as Paul's group reached the eighteenth.

Occasionally someone would comment on the conditions of the fairway or the greens—"Best I've seen this year," said Paul. But no one mentioned the personal stakes, which were different for each golfer.

Unlike their younger counterparts on the regular tour—"the Junior Tour," one of the older players sarcastically called it; "the snotnoses," said senior veteran Dick Rhyan, whose son was then an aspiring pro—most of these men had experienced the vicissitudes of life. One had worked in a steel mill for a time, another had overcome cancer. They hadn't gone to college on golf scholarships. But they talked very little about their lives, as though this were somehow bad form.

"Why do you keep asking about pressure?" Paul asked after his round. "Everyone's got pressure. My friend's got pressure in his business. He's got to make the mortgage payments on his building. That's pressure."

His words, like his manner now, seemed part of a very human, very understandable pose, part of the patter that masks tension on the course wherever competitive golf is played. Sometimes he told a joke himself, just to keep up with the guys, but his weren't delivered with the panache of Still's. Or he'd spin a golf anecdote.

"This is the course where I played in the Massachusetts Open in 1981. Finished second." (He won that title the year before, along with the New England Open and New England PGA Championship.)

"Man, you've got to be supple to play this game," he said. He was feeling not just tired but disappointed, as if his aging body were letting him down. "I feel like I'm one hundred years old," he said. "Two times fifty."

Later, as the afternoon sun baked down on the thick fairways (freshly mowed to a height of three-eighths of an inch), Paul put his clubs in the trunk of his friend's Volvo and was soon on his way for dinner at his mother's in Haverhill. He certainly didn't stick around for the golf clinic Chi Chi Rodriguez conducted at the practice tee. It was almost as if he were an outsider in a world he'd been trying to be part of all his professional life. Complaining of a pinched nerve in his neck, Rodriguez turned over most of the clinic to his colleague Bob Brue, but not without entertaining the crowd with some poor one-liners.

"I agree with Bob Hope," said Chi Chi. "I think if someone wants to burn the American flag he should go ahead. But he should put himself inside that flag before he lights it." It was a sentiment that would be endorsed in most professional golf locker rooms, where the political climate is conservative and few question a status quo that rewards them, sometimes lavishly.

Few players hit balls on the practice tee after the clinic. A lone golfer practiced his stroke on the putting green, using one of the new, long putters that had enabled some of the older golfers to remain competitive. "I wouldn't use one," claimed Moran. "It's not a golf stroke."

Some of Moran's fellow competitors returned to the clubhouse for the dinner held for the pro-am participants. Like so many other perks—golf balls, golf shoes, even bottles of anti-balding lotion—the food was free to the pros. They did pay for their motel rooms, however, a fact of their lives that most of them grumbled about, unless they were among the elite who could afford to live luxuriously on the road, traveling as Chi Chi did in his own plane.

Paul Moran would never buy a plane from his golf winnings at Nashawtuc.

TEEING OFF IN the first round of the tournament proper on Friday, Moran hit first, somehow an appropriate honor for the only Boston-area player then on the Senior Tour. He was wearing tan pants and a white knit shirt. Squat and compact, he nevertheless generated tremendous power in his swing. Some of that energy came from the muscular forearms, but there had to be tremendous leg strength as well. Moran had the build of a fullback and the wary eyes of a blackjack dealer. When he posed for a picture he lost the smile he kept on the tee or while he was walking between shots. In a formal portrait his suntanned face betrayed a weariness that was less apparent when he was competing and still could dream of turning his life around with the next shot.

It was just after eight o'clock, and he'd been up since six-thirty on this clear, warm summer morning. A dozen or so people were watching Moran and his threesome. Included in the small gathering of onlookers was Paul's Uncle Bill from Haverhill. Uncle Bill, who was also Paul's godfather, caddied for his nephew when he won the New England Open, one of many regional professional events. He was a friendly, outgoing man who struck up conversations with everyone in the gallery. He was rooting hard for his nephew, and Moran would stay in the Haverhill area an extra day after the tournament ended to play a round of golf with Uncle Bill.

Moran's drive on the par-four first hole, 387 yards in length, landed perfectly, in the center of the fairway, about 150 yards from the green. A nice iron shot brought him to that green, about twenty feet from the flagstick, and with two putts he had his par. The pattern continued through the next three holes. Then, on the par-five fifth, he pushed his drive past a clump of trees on the right side of the fairway and elected to play his next shot along the trees, in the adjacent fairway of the third hole, coming back over the trees to the correct green on his third shot.

This strategy worked, and Paul recovered on the hole with another par. But something else had happened that, perhaps, rattled his concentration ever so slightly. On the same hole, one of his opponents also had pushed his drive right, but the ball hadn't cleared the trees. Taking a practice stroke, the other player inadvertently hit his ball, which landed under another tree. A poor third shot hit yet another tree, and the player eventually took an eight on the hole—a snowman, in golfer's parlance. The man was furious with himself and thereafter played with what Paul would describe as a case of a golfing malaise called "I don't give a shit."

The ethic of golf prevented Paul from commenting, in part because the men all realize they must live together on the road. But golfers also suffer such misfortune in silence because they are ever fearful that a similar fate might lurk ahead for them. Indeed, on the very next hole Paul put his approach on the green and proceeded to leave his first putt short. He stepped over the ball, his posture bent, and he pushed the second putt a few feet past the hole.

The silence seemed the foil for an inaudible gasp. Everyone stood still.

Paul squatted over his ball again. He took the head of his Ping B-60 putter back and moved it forward. The stroke seemed hurried, and the result was yet another missed putt.

"He went to sleep," explained Mobile later.

Paul's ball now lay where it had after his first putt, but he'd wasted two strokes putting the ball past the hole and back again. He finally made the fourth, but this big lapse in concentration separated him then from the men who succeeded on the Senior Tour and, coupled with other mistakes, cost him thousands of dollars.

"You play this game long enough, anything will happen to you," Paul said afterward. "You can show up to play at the wrong course. I've had that happen." It was a candid admission, the kind that won sympathy, but impossible to imagine a player such as Greg Norman ever making. Someone once asked Jack Nicklaus how he had made so many pressure putts in his career. "In my mind I never missed one," he answered.

Resolutely, philosophically, Paul worked to forget the four putts. But you can't *work* to forget such mistakes, like the triple bogey in Phoenix. The painful lesson of professional golf is that you simply forget them—or they will haunt you forever. But they had marred his round, leaving a blemish that only some birdies could have banished. Though he hit several more excellent shots, his only deviation from par through the next several holes was a bogey on the fourteenth, a dogleg where his drive landed in a fairway bunker. Paul made up that lost stroke with a lone birdie at eighteen, so his score for the day came in at two over par—not the kind of number that was going to put him in position for a good check that week.

"Well, Mobile," said Paul, "I think I'll hit some balls later." That message meant Mobile was supposed to stick around, scrounging a lunch coupon from someone if he could, while Paul relaxed in the clubhouse filled with members and guests enjoying drinks and the biggest bowl of shrimp at least one of those guests had ever seen in his life. Paul would meet Mobile at some indeterminate time later on the practice range. Mobile nodded his head and disappeared with Paul's bag. Paul headed into the lounge to cool off with a Perrier and talk with a local newspaper reporter. But first he splashed some cold water on his face and combed his thinning hair. Over his shoulders he draped a light orange sweater, while Mobile stood by in the same clothes he'd been wearing all day.

Patiently, Paul recited the familiar story of his near brush with fame in Phoenix to the reporter.

"When did you first break ninety?" the reporter asked.

"I never shot *over* ninety," Paul responded tartly.

Despite this bit of boasting, the interview never turned into the ego trip that such occasions so often are for professional athletes. Partly, that was because golf is such a humbling game. Even the best golfers in the world mysteriously lose their touch on a given day and can't putt, or can't drive—can't, sometimes, do any of the things that usually seem to come so effortlessly.

But there was another reason for Paul's modesty, having less to do with the 74 he had shot today and much more to do with the fact that in his fifties he was still waiting for everything in his golf game to come together. At that age, even in golf, it might have been wise to ask whether it ever would. But anyone who felt that way would not be in Paul Moran's spikes.

Listening in on some of the interview was a part of his retinue, Paul's childhood friend Joe D'Orazio, a successful businessman and once a semipro baseball player. D'Orazio started playing golf when he was twenty-six, and partly through lessons from Paul he currently carried a handicap of eight, meaning his average score was about 80.

After the interview, Paul excused himself, telling D'Orazio he'd meet him at the practice tee.

"There," Paul said upon his return from the bathroom. "I feel great." He had the kind of excessive concern with his body of any athlete.

It was the game he talked about now as he hit iron shots for D'Orazio and John Schlee, another golfer on the Senior Tour. Next to Schlee, former San Francisco 49ers quarterback John Brody, also a senior golfer, hit balls, too.

"I'm out here trying to figure something out," said Moran to Schlee. "When I'm playing my best, I can fade the ball with a hook swing." It was a conversation that Billy Harmon's father would have followed with relish. Moran meant he could set up to hit the ball with a left curve, a hook, yet have it work to the right, a fade. The talk continued to get more technical. D'Orazio listened in, hoping to pick up a tip that would help his own game.

Paul hit another shot, which curved to the right before it landed, just as it was supposed to.

"You can talk to a fade, but a hook won't listen," he said, quoting Lee Trevino. The shot he'd just hit was a fade, but he didn't talk to it. He admired it in silence while D'Orazio did the talking.

"Oh, that was strong, Paul, that was strong."

Then Paul spoke.

"That's as good as I can hit it," he announced with consuming satisfaction.

"Paul's the best tee-to-green player out here, huh?" D'Orazio asked rhetorically, with forgivable exaggeration.

"You shoot a score here and the whole country knows about it," said Schlee. This, too, was grand overstatement, but no one disputed Schlee. The practice range was a place to work on one's game, but it also inspired hope. You could hit shots there that you couldn't in the pressure of a tournament. More than anything else, the difference between success on the range and on the course defined the difference between Paul Moran and Homero Blancas, or, on a different level, between Blancas in his prime and Greg Norman. Thousands of golfers had a swing that could, at least on occasion on the range, produce good shots. But very few men could duplicate their effort in tournament play.

"That was crushed," Paul beamed at another three-iron. "That was crushed hard."

Paul stopped to explain another nuance to D'Orazio. He mentioned the swing of Gary Player, one of the most famous golfers in history, now a Senior Tour marquee player. D'Orazio nodded his head.

Then, looking up, looking along the row of other golfers on the sunlit range, Paul focused his gaze on the man at the opposite end of the range from himself and, barely masking his satisfaction that the two of them were doing the same thing in the same place, that they were indeed part of the same profession, said with his voice rising:

"There's Gary now."

SHARKBITE

THERE'S A TOTALLY different side to life when you become successful.

People don't realize how busy I am behind the scenes. That's because I like to be in a hands-on basis, just like my golf game. I've got a lot of feel in my golf game in the way I teach myself. And it's the same with business. I want to be involved with the business so I can know what's happening inside my office.

I DO ALL the things the sports psychologists say to do. But I'm self-taught in that respect. I've read a lot, I understand that stuff. I do it naturally myself.

I'm not against kids going for outside help. If someone has a problem with their golf swing, they go to a teacher to fix it. If they have problems with their mind, they have to get help to fix that too. And there's nothing wrong with that.

The thing is, if you can get all those assets working for you, then you've got to be one or two steps ahead of everybody else. I personally think that the younger players rely on outside help too early in their career.

Growing up, I think you have to understand the nuances of the game, you have to figure out for yourself where you went wrong, what were you feeling during that time. You can correct that sort of thing yourself. I don't like to see a kid of twenty or twenty-one years old being told how to play the game of golf in his head by a guy who can't even play the game.

Just because you're a sports psychologist, you can't tell a twenty-year-old who's raring to go on the first tee, 'Hey, take your time, hit a one-iron off the tee, put it in this position, go there.' You have to be able to play your own game. And the only way to be able to do that is by playing a long time. And if that doesn't work after a couple of years and you feel you can't get up to the next level, *then* you go to somebody.

WALKING
THE
COURSE

WHETHER YOU ARE playing or watching, golf creates a level of focus and concentration that obliterates everything else. It is as though you are taking an encapsulated vacation in a world where you have very little impact on your environment except for one preeminent activity: hitting your golf ball (or watching someone else hit it). The game is very hard, but for brief periods of time—sometimes only a shot or a hole, sometimes a round or an entire tournament—a golfer can feel he has the upper hand on the game, that as Greg Norman says he is controlling it rather than it controlling him. This is the source of the game's addictive quality, the fleeting feeling of power it bequeaths to a player. And then it is gone, usually as mysteriously as it came; and so the player returns to the range or calls his coach or his wife or simply hits the road to the next tournament. At the professional level, tournament golf and tournament life are related. Golf is context, and the context of the professional tour is a course called the road.

FRONT NINE

1. Getting into the Clubhouse

THOUGH THE WAITING list for tickets has been closed for years, you can get into the Masters if you really want to. The men who run the world's most prestigious golf tournament want you to think you must be at least a distant cousin of founder Bobby Jones. They are selective about whom they let into their plantation. They don't like CBS television announcer Gary McCord, or his predecessor, Jack Whitaker, one of the most respected men in his business. They don't want the front nine televised. And they certainly don't want just anybody walking through the front gate. But you can get in if you're willing to risk a little embarrassment, if you've got the cash or the right connections.

South of Augusta, Georgia, State Highway 25 suddenly becomes a four-lane highway, sprouting shopping plazas and fast-food restaurants as it nears the intersection with a road named after the founder of the Augusta National Golf Club, Bobby Jones.

By Sunday, many of the Masters fans have had their fill of peach cobbler and were heading home early. Though there are strict prohibitions against this, calling for expulsion from the list of season badge holders to anyone caught, quite a few of those people scalped their badges before they left. All you had to do was look around in the vicinity of a restaurant across Washington Road from the club. Imitating the symbol of a Masters victory that was presented to the tournament winner each year, the restaurant was called the Green Jacket.

A girl waving a sign that read "Parking $10" directed drivers into the large lot of a shopping plaza. It was easy to know which direction to walk. All you had to do was follow the crowd, which had the feeling of early arrivals at a country fair. A friendly older man wearing a plaid sport jacket and carrying a yellow sweater said he was from Kentucky. Yes, of course he attended *the* Derby.

Ahead, the traffic was thickening and slowing almost to a standstill. It wasn't long before a tall, large man responded to inquisitive looks with a steady stare.

"Help you?" he asked.

What if he was an undercover policeman? Security was very tight, and scalpers were reportedly prosecuted. The imperious Masters committee was so strict about enforcing tournament policies that after Jack Whitaker referred to the tournament crowd as a mob he had been removed from his duties. More recently, Gary McCord had come under fire from Masters officials—and from Tom Watson, who penned a sour letter—for humorous remarks that were considered inappropriate. McCord's patter would eventually earn him an expulsion, after he described the greens as being so fast they must have been treated with "bikini wax," which caused the world's best golfers to miss so many putts they had to be taken away in body bags. As if the issue were one of life and death, Tom Watson would write the chairman of the Masters, urging that McCord be banned, and he was. In the future, McCord said, he would spend Masters week in New Zealand, "bungee jumping buck naked except for a Masters cap on my head."

"How much?" a customer asked the man.

"Buck and a quarter."

The customer counted out seven twenties and gave them to the man, saying he didn't have the correct change.

"No," the man replied. "That's just right, sir. Rest is a tip."

2. Customs of Etiquette and Decorum

IN THE WHOLE world, there is probably not a more famous golf tournament than the Masters, which since its inception in

1934 has been played in April at the same golf course, the one Robert Tyre Jones, Jr., began.

"In golf, customs of etiquette and decorum are just as important as rules governing play," Jones once wrote. He was a good writer, too, with a Harvard law degree, though his diction could give his prose too patrician a tone. "It is appropriate for spectators to applaud successful strokes in proportion to difficulty but excessive demonstrations by a player or his partisans is not proper because of the possible effect upon other competitors.

"Most distressing to those who love the game of golf is the applauding or cheering of misplays or misfortunes of a player. Such occurrences have been rare at the Masters but we must eliminate them entirely if our patrons are to continue to merit their reputation as the most knowledgeable and considerate in the world."

The presumably unintended hauteur of those remarks, reprinted in the spectator booklets given to Masters badge holders—patrons, as Jones had called them, or "our spectator friends"—betray the high regard in which the Masters folks hold themselves. The Masters is a tournament with such a reputation for success that in another of its publications it explains its public relations policy as if the media were an adjunct of the club. "The Club handles its public relations by merely supplying factual material to the sportswriters, commentators, and telecasters." The media, that policy implies, are one of the Masters committees composed of the Captains of Industry who parade proudly during Masters week in their green jackets, sworn to write or say only good things about the green-jacketed Captains and their golf course (which the lucky few are permitted to play via a media lottery after the tournament).

3. Shark Dreams

SINCE THE 1993 Players Championship concluded two weeks before, there had been just one tournament played in the interim, the Freeport-McMoran Golf Classic in New Orleans. A relative newcomer on the tour, Mike Standly, had won that event, thereby earning himself the last exemption into the Masters. Brad Faxon had not competed, but the Shark had finished fourth in a tournament he had nearly won the year before. In 1990, when it was called the USF&G Classic, he had lost to David Frost when Frost holed his last shot from a bunker.

But there is no tournament Norman wants to win more than the Masters, where he has finished second twice, both times by a single stroke. Going into the final 1993 round, he stood at three under par in a tie for eighth place, a distant six strokes behind the leader, Bernhard Langer. This was not an insurmountable number for Norman to make up; he often shoots very low fourth-round scores. And Augusta, with its superslick greens and its wide fairways, is suited to his game, with its emphasis on long, accurate driving and excellent putting.

4. Just the Fax

PAIRED WITH NORMAN in the finale was Faxon, who was playing in only his second Masters. Though Cubby insisted today was "just another round of golf," Faxon was wearing the same red shirt he had worn during the fourth round in his Pleasant Valley victory the year before. He wanted to do well.

Faxon's family, many of whom had made the trip to Augusta for the tournament, would be rooting him on. Their presence made Brad's tournament play into frequent mini-reunions. His father or mother might walk a round, or his sister Lee; at another tournament an aunt might be present. So faithfully and happily do these people attend that it sometimes seems Brad's purpose in golf is to give pleasure to those around him, to share his good fortune with those closest to him. A Faxon gallery often takes on the complexion of a roving party.

Brad's four-year-old daughter, Melanie, would be absent today, with an arm in a cast. The night before, Melanie, who is

Faxon's older daughter—the younger, Emily, was not quite two—had broken the arm in a fall. Dodie, the girls' nanny, would watch her today. The girls and Brad's wife, Bonnie, whom he had met as a Furman University student, still traveled with him, as they had since the girls were babies. Though this was not a substitute for being at home together, it provided more than a semblance of family life. When he could, Brad rented a house near a tournament site rather than hotel rooms. And he plunged into the care of his girls when he was with them, getting up in the middle of the night to take care of them, even if he had an early tee time the next morning. But this nomadic routine would end in little more than a year, when Melanie was old enough for kindergarten. In anticipation of that event, the Faxons had decided to move back to Rhode Island, where the schools were better. After that, the girls would be able to travel with their father only during school vacations, which would make their separations longer and therefore harder.

Of course, for every player who could afford such relative luxuries there were many who could not or would not spend more than the minimum on the road. Australian Brett Ogle was a notorious budgeter, insisting that all a man needed was a room with a bed, a bathroom, and a television. Greg Norman, on the other hand, flew from tournament to tournament in his own jet, as if to demonstrate that how a player performed was how he traveled. Much of the expense could be written off, but this seemed less important than the demonstration that a star must live like a star. Adding cachet to his own perks, Norman had also sold his previous jet to good friend and fellow star Nick Price, the victor at the Players Championship.

"Daddy," Melanie asked Brad one day, "couldn't you get another job instead of golf?"

Now, to an old Rhode Island friend waiting for him when he emerged from the plantation-style Augusta clubhouse, Faxon talked briefly and cheerfully about such matters. It is one of the distinguishing features of his personality that at moments of high stress in his work he can concentrate for a moment on an autograph request or a question about hockey or baseball, two other sports he loves, or a brief exchange about the day.

Once, during a pro-am round at a course surrounded by condominiums and houses, he initiated a conversation with a young fan waiting by a tee. The boy was on his bike, and Faxon asked if he could borrow it.

"Sure!" said the kid, as if the prospect of the bicycle's use by a fairly famous professional athlete was somehow going to add a new dimension to its importance in his life.

Faxon looked ahead of his golfing group to the golfers who had just teed off. They were still waiting to hit their second shots, which meant his, Faxon's, group would have to wait before they could hit their drives off the tee. So he had a few minutes. Faxon hopped on the boy's bike, which was much too small for him to pedal comfortably, and rode around the tee in a circle.

Often while playing in tournament rounds he sees someone he knows in the gallery. Invariably he says hello, usually by name. He is very good at remembering names. He can remember the names of people he played with in pro-ams several years ago. Some of them, such as actor Joe Pesci and Donald Trump, are celebrities, and Faxon may use the time with them on the course to schmooze or trade a golf lesson for an investment tip. Many are business people whose company has contributed enough to the tournament to entitle them to a pro-am spot. Of course, these people remember Brad. They look for him the next year, when the tournament at which they met is contested again. Or they write him, as do his fans. A couple in Michigan wrote him to say how much something Brad had said to their son meant. A grandmother of a young fan in Massachusetts keeps an autographed Brad Faxon golf card on her refrigerator and regularly checks the tournament standings on television each week, to see how he is doing.

With outward ease and a relative lack of self-absorption, Faxon basically understands his place in the relationship of a public figure and his public. Like most of his tour colleagues, he wants or needs some protection from that public; interlopers must earn trustworthiness, must through some signification of dress and background and manner pass scrutiny.

Also like his colleagues, Faxon can be guilty of mistaking a polite inquiry about his health for a probing question about his golf game. You can ask him how he is after a round and he may reply, "I really hit the ball solid today. Hooked my drive on two, but otherwise my ball-striking was excellent. Then there was a long putt at thirteen. . . ." At such times of golfing recitation, Faxon or other tour members can seem like children talking about what happened to them at school. But for Faxon this is the exception in his speech. Usually he wants to talk about someone else, something else. A musical group or a recent incident on the road, even a new style of shoes.

5. His Hugeness

FAXON'S PLAYING PARTNER today, Greg Norman, rarely in public is able to transcend himself in this way, so that the focus of any such public conversation in which he participates is invariably himself. For the most part this reflects the different stage Norman occupies.

Certainly he is the tour's most charismatic figure. Only the long-hitting, bad-behaving John Daly has ever attracted larger tournament galleries. Everywhere Norman goes on a golf course, large numbers of people follow. Here at the Masters today, as soon as he arrived at the clubhouse, riding in a golf cart with his wife, Laura, there was a stir.

"There *he* is!" fans said to one another. *"The Shar-ark."*

And they would push forward to get closer, hoping he might sign an autograph or walk past them closely enough that the loose cloth of his blue-and-black shirt might brush theirs. No other golfer at the tournament played before people who were wearing clothes and hats with the insignia that represented his nickname. Faxon himself understood this, once exclaiming to a reporter over the fuss Norman caused wherever he went and whatever he did, "Greg's *huge.*"

This "hugeness," defined in part by Norman's estimated annual income of around $10 million, can be intimidating to competitors, many of whom, such as former British Open champion Ian Baker-Finch, admit they try to play their best when they are paired with Greg. Faxon has played with him often and, on occasion, beaten him, most recently at the Tournament of Champions in January, when he finished in a tie for fifth against Norman's tie for twelfth. In a very well played round in Great Britain in December, he narrowly missed beating Norman in match play.

Part of Faxon's confidence in playing with Norman comes from his putting, which is at least the equal of Norman's. But a deeper, more fundamental measure of his assurance is his realization, schooled over many years in countless rounds of golf, that he isn't playing against Greg Norman. Their mutual opponent is the course, or the game itself, and they both realize this, a fact Faxon is better at remembering than some of the other men who have tried to succeed at this game.

6. Golf Action

THE FIRST HOLE at Augusta, an uphill, slight dogleg par four of 400 yards, requires a tee shot of 247 yards to carry a bunker on the right side of the fairway. Such a distance means little to a player of Greg Norman's length off the tee, and his drive landed almost at the gallery crosswalk, at least fifty yards past the bunker and about forty yards farther than Brad Faxon's.

Faxon's subsequent long shot into the two-tiered green triggered trouble, and his three-putt earned him a bogey. Norman missed a birdie putt of about ten feet and tapped in for par.

Faxon got another five on the next hole, a difficult, downhill par five, with the pin set above the right-side bunker. Norman, laying up with his second shot, sculled his third, over the bunker and the green. Then, chipping downhill, he holed his fourth shot for a birdie that inspired a huge roar from the people standing behind him and around the backside of the green. Perhaps, as he had so often in the past, the Shark would go on a birdie run, getting himself back into contention in the tournament.

Instead, Norman played the next twelve holes in a shocking six over par, while Faxon mixed three more bogeys to go with two birdies. This placed the two men three strokes apart, with Faxon having the advantage, when they came to the fifteenth tee, the last of Augusta's par fives and the second in a span of three holes easily reachable in two shots.

Norman birdied the fifteenth, only to give back the stroke with a bogey at the following hole. Faxon, who also birdied fifteen, hit his tee shot at sixteen into a bunker above and to the right of the hole. Then to another mighty Augusta roar he scored a birdie by holing his bunker shot, made especially difficult because water lay beyond the green. When the ball went in, Faxon threw his Titleist visor several feet into the air. The sound of the roar that greeted his shot echoed through the tall pines lining so many of the course's beautifully manicured hills, the fairway grass mowed by a phalanx of men on machines, each evening after play, to a height of three-eighths of an inch, the sweep of dogwoods and azaleas on the steeper hills behind the thirteenth green and alongside sixteen and elsewhere tended by unseen minions who work all year; in fact, some of the busiest working months at the course are in the summer, when the course is closed for play.

7. Knowledgeable Crowds

AS THE CROWD awaited Chip Beck's second shot on fifteen, it wondered how he could lay up there when he was three behind Langer. It was quiet away from the crowd, reverently described on television by veteran announcer Ken Venturi as the most knowledgeable in golf. A former U.S. Open champion, Venturi is always making such superlative claims in a syntax that borrows heavily from Casey Stengel's. Rarely does a week of CBS televised golf pass without Venturi or one of his partners praising the ground crew or the Goodyear blimp captain or the fans.

Within this center of capitalism, there seemed more than the hint of a hustle underneath the veneer of the dogwoods. Here, in golf's equivalent of Versailles, resided the proud vestiges of a moneyed world that still stands as the sporting equivalent of the business machinery that makes it work. Bobby Jones may have had a visionary's dream, but it was money that turned it into fairways and greens, just as money makes possible this annual gathering of the golfing faithful in Augusta.

Here, in modern, air-conditioned offices located in a new building tastefully set back from the course and partially hidden by the arcade where so many of the patrons entered and picnicked on pimiento sandwiches and Coke served in plain green-and-white paper cups, the business of the Masters is conducted during the tournament behind Pinkerton-guarded doors. Indeed, there are Pinkerton guards everywhere, which has to account at least partially for the crowd behavior that so moved Venturi. If you litter at the Masters, a Pinkerton guard will speak to you about your bad manners. If you run across a fairway at a crosswalk, a "gallery guard" will warn you politely not to do so again. This guard, dressed in his civilian clothes with only a yellow hard hat as uniform, will be giving his time to the tournament in exchange for the privilege of watching some of the golf when his duties are completed. Two guards on the seventeenth have been coming for more than ten years. They use vacation days at work and spend their own money to stay in a private home listed with the Masters housing bureau so they don't have to commute back and forth from their homes in Columbia, South Carolina. The housing bureau, an adjunct of the local chamber of commerce, matches people looking for a place to stay with people who have rooms to rent (or the whole house might be for rent, just during Masters week; the owners then spend the week elsewhere).

Like many activities associated with the Masters, the housing bureau is run without the aid of a computer. This contributes to the tournament's folksy charm. The Captains of Industry flaunt their green jackets, greeting workers on a first-name basis while being addressed in return by their surnames, preceded of course by the word "Mister." If you call a member of the club by phone and he isn't in his room, chances are good that the receptionist will know where on the grounds he is. He might be in the grillroom, for example; and if you ask to be connected there the employee who answers the phone will know definitively if he is enjoying a drink or sandwich, the way a person does when someone calls a person at his or her home.

8. Members of the Club

INDEED, FOR MANY members of the club, Masters week takes on the aura of a return home, which is especially revealing since so few of the members actually come from the area of Augusta. They hail, instead, from New England and Texas and the West Coast. They have work to do at the Masters, some of it fairly responsible work, such as serving on the club's television committee. Nevertheless, Masters week seems more like a vacation for most of them.

They have cocktails with friends. They sneak off to play golf elsewhere, which must look like slumming it to some of them. After all, their own course is so exclusive that a writer, invited to watch the tournament as the paying guest of a member, was told when he asked about possibly playing the course, "Not a chance, not . . . a . . . chance," whereupon the member, his host, hung up the phone on him.

117

9. King Cotton

FOR MOST OF the players, the Masters is a favored spot because the field is limited, the magnificent course is in magnificent shape, and it is more difficult during the Masters for interlopers to bother the players. Even writers with the proper credentials can't talk with players on the practice tee, and autograph-seeking by fans is permitted only on the Washington Road side of the clubhouse.

That road, or the very fact of its existence, makes the course seem an especially astonishing anomaly, for it is filled with the same strip attractions of highways throughout America: fast food, gas station, convenience store. The road is so close to the course that a huge screen has been erected at the road end of the driving range so the pros won't knock their practice shots into someone's windshield.

Several miles down that road, which when the course was built on the site of a former nursery must have been a quaint, quiet connection between countryside and city, Augusta's core has been undergoing an urban revival of sorts, with a spiffy new riverside development of condos and a hotel near shops and storefronts, many deserted, on tree-lined Broad Street, a commercial center whose heyday, more than one hundred years ago, was made possible by King Cotton. Augusta is a city that prospered during plantation times, its prominent white people the beneficiaries of America's pre–Civil War system of slavery.

No slaves now, of course, but no surplus of black men and women either at Augusta National, which has exactly two black members (exactly twice the number of black Americans currently active on the PGA Tour, though that particular man had not qualified to play in this year's Masters). There were a few black fans at the tournament, but for the most part this was a white man's world, "cracker heaven," one fan called it. Until only a few years ago, Masters contestants had to take a club caddy, and virtually all those caddies were black. That has changed; the pros now can bring their own caddies, virtually all of whom are white—and well paid (with a typical 5 to 10 percent of a player's earnings on top of a basic weekly stipend).

While the present descendants of Augusta can not be blamed for building the cotton warehouses of the past, the grounds there still have the feel of exclusion if not prejudice. And while this exclusion turns as much on class as it does on race, today it is impossible to imagine a tournament being started in the South with a name that conjures up the worst images of the past.

Masters.

Massah.

BACK NINE

10. Amen Corner

MANY MASTERS PATRONS were missing the final holes of tournament play. After his birdie at fifteen, it was a foregone conclusion that Langer was going to win. Would Beck hold on to second? No one shopping for souvenirs in the arcade by the "patron corridor" discussed the question. Snacking on one of the outdoor benches was a man wearing a straw Shark hat on his head and a *Playboy* bunny earring in one earlobe. At three over par, his man had not finished well: Norman's score for the day was 75, and his four-day total of 290 placed him in a tie for thirty-first. The Shark had stalked the game today; three times on three consecutive back-nine holes he had fired over water to reach well-protected pins; each of those three shots had found the water. With business and personal obligations elsewhere, he would leave Augusta today for a six-week hiatus from the tour, nicely perched in third place on the year's money-winning list, just ahead of Nick Price, who had followed up his Players Championship victory two weeks ago by missing the two-day Masters cut.

At the tenth tee, adjacent to the eighteenth green, a few solitary fans walked in the direction of Amen Corner, the three holes that form a kind of turn on the back nine and that usually set up whatever disaster or triumph is experienced by the golfers in contention each year in the final round. Indeed, after falling behind today, the Shark went bogey, double bogey, bogey on the eleventh, twelfth, and thirteenth holes, shooting at pins with an abandon rare even for him but necessary if he was to have any chance of catching the leaders, which he failed to do.

The eleventh green, where Raymond Floyd's second shot in a playoff with Nick Faldo three years before had landed in the small pond by the green, ending Floyd's bid for a second Masters, was tantalizingly close to the place behind the gallery ropes, also marking off the twelfth tee. A Pinkerton guard stood in the trees along the nearby thirteenth fairway.

The only sound was the many birds singing in the trees. Then, from a distance, the sound of fans, whose applause had to be greeting Langer and Beck as they came up the eighteenth.

Before this place was a golf course, and before it was a nursery, it was a plantation. Where was the voice of Massah and where were the vanished voices of the men whose forced, backbreaking labor it had been to clear this land before it could be tilled?

The birds sang at the tee of the par-three twelfth, where only an hour or so earlier Dan Forsman had taken a *seven*, thereby ending any hopes he had of owning a green jacket this year. He had known that by the time he crossed gentle Raes Creek on a footbridge named after Ben Hogan, returning for his tee shot on thirteen via the Byron Nelson Bridge. A lonely walk.

BYRON NELSON, EIGHTY-TWO, who won eleven tournaments in a row in 1945, would hold court in the foyer of the press building the day before the start of the 1994 Masters. Because of a bad hip he needed a cane to walk, and this prevented him from taking a full swing in the opening ceremony the next morning on the first tee. But he still showed up, along with Sam Snead and ninety-two-year-old Gene Sarazen, and all three men hit shots. Snead's, in fact, traveled a good two hundred yards.

The enormously popular Nelson wasn't happy with the outcome of surgery he'd had on his leg, but he refused to complain. "I'm not like that," he said. His handshake was still vigorous, and what enormous hands he had. It was easy to imagine them making a toy of a golf club.

Nelson greeted Ted Danforth, a longtime Augusta member whose father was a member before him. When he came to the tournament, Danforth stayed in a cottage attached to the clubhouse, kind of an Augusta condo, though it wasn't called that. His wife, Laura, a tanned, black-haired woman who had spent most of the past month on Long Island Sound, had just arrived. She was deeply dismayed to discover that the refrigerator had only grapefruit juice and milk in it. A friend came by, a man who was part owner of the Atlanta Falcons, and with him was the recently retired head of the Leo J. Burnett advertising agency in Chicago. They talked about how one of them didn't have the appropriate pass to get into the parking lot, but had managed to sneak his way in. They talked football. And both of the men talked a little bit about their golf games, while Mrs. Danforth, a perfect hostess, politely listened.

Later, her husband returned from a round of golf and took a writer on a tour of the grounds. They had a sandwich in the pressroom, just an egg salad sandwich, which was free if you were a credentialed reporter at the Masters. Danforth insisted the writer have a sandwich.

Mac O'Grady presided under the oak tree by the back of the clubhouse. O'Grady, who had needed seventeen attempts to receive his tour card, had an undistinguished tour career, during which he won the Greater Hartford Open. He had now become the teacher of the great Spanish player and British Open winner Seve Ballesteros, who had twice won the Masters but lately had lost his stroke.

O'Grady was trying to argue that there were several tour players who used beta blockers as a way of combating performance anxiety. This charge, reported in the daily press, was met with skepticism and outright denial by players, most of whom insist that any kind of performance-altering drug is ineffective in helping a person play golf at this level because the slightest change in the calibration of a person's nerves or physiology has a profound impact on his game. Nick Price did admit to having taken beta blockers because of a high-blood-pressure condition, which is actually what the medicine is prescribed for, but had stopped taking them.

AFTER THE 1993 Masters, the Normans headed west to vacation in tony Beaver Creek, a few miles down the road from Vail. But Greg wasn't planning to ski. He preferred to drive a snowmobile in the Rockies at eighty miles per hour.

One evening during their vacation the Normans stopped at a place with great Mexican food called the Saloon in Minturn, an old mining town. The Shark signed a photograph of himself that went up on the wall, next to the photographs of movie stars and musicians.

11. On the Road Again

LEAVING AUGUSTA, THE traffic was not so bad if your route was initially back into town, away from the interstate to the north. Outside Savannah, you pick up I-95 at the intersection with I-16, a good place to stop for gas. It's a four-hour drive to the coast, where you pass a sign for a Gary Player–designed golf course near the causeway connecting the mainland and Hilton Head, with outlet stores that welcome visitors to this island of extraordinary natural beauty. Gradually the outlets turn to boutiques, and there are signs along the way for fancy golf courses and posh resorts, and, past the corner where a TGIF restaurant stands, midst the rich dark green foliage of the South Carolina coastal spring, the brightly lit sign for the Days Inn motel.

12. Morning Coffee

THE NEXT MORNING, Monday morning in Hilton Head, South Carolina, the April sun rising over miles of wide ocean beach, the sweet scent of brewed coffee coming from the dining room of the Days Inn.

Yes, thanks. I'll sit outside.

Where's the coffee? . . . I'll serve myself.

Do you sell newspapers here? Ma'am?

Monday morning at the Days Inn, the dead bugs on the pool's surface, the early sun's reflection off the rental car's hood, the scent of jasmine. Memories of a man at the bar last night, an old golfer, he must have been in his eighties, dictating his memoirs over a martini:

"It was just after the war, and the tour was getting going again.

"I left the city on the coldest morning of the winter. I'll never forget the train station that day, the sky over the station so blue and the snow along all the tracks still fresh from a storm the night before. What clouds of steam the waiting locomotives let out!

"I can still see the bent-over figure of a switchman in the cold, snowy yard, banging with some sort of tool on a switch that apparently wouldn't open or close. What a shattering sound that banging must have made, but I didn't hear it. I was inside the passenger car then, impatiently waiting for the start of a journey that would take me west, all the way to the warm coast.

"There were some tournaments being played there, but I

wasn't thinking about the money they paid. It wouldn't be the official prizes I was after. I golfed for much bigger stakes than that."

MONDAY MORNING, BUT no Monday morning paper. Find something else to read.
"April 1993 WHERE TO GO Hilton Head Island."
Coffee's cold. Where's my breakfast?
What's the rush?

"WHAT YOU'LL SEE: These four tours will give you an overview of the Island, so you can find your way around more easily during your visit. You'll pass all the major shopping centers, marinas, and plantations. Each plantation is a showplace of beautiful homes and gardens. They are private residential communities, although most have restaurants, marinas, shopping areas and/or recreational facilities. **All have gates at the entrance to the residential areas and you will not be permitted to tour these areas unless you make arrangements with the security official near the main gate.** Guards will not issue passes for 'just looking,' so be prepared to name your destination when you stop at the gate for your pass."

DRIVING TO HARBOUR Town, just down the road. Harbour Town Golf Links, Sea Pines Plantation.
Sea Pines.
Bicycle paths.
Golf courses left and right.
Cute little shopping center.
Beautiful homes and gardens.
At the gate the guard checked parking passes before waving visitors on through. The traffic was pretty light, no one driving in a hurry. There was no reason to drive in a hurry here at Sea Pines Plantation. Anyone who is in a hurry here has come to the wrong place.

You had to pass another guard. *"Just looking."* Then you followed the directions of yet another guard about getting into the parking lot to which you had been assigned, and you looked for a space underneath a tree, keeping a watchful eye on other cars and ruts in the unpaved lot, what in plantation-worldview must be designated as vacant land, which was terribly hard to fathom in this land of six-figure prices for homesites but also not a question you planned to fathom further as you locked the rental car and purposefully walked in the direction of the television and equipment trailers that were a bustling exciting sure sign of the tournament's location.

13. Monday morning

ANYONE WHOSE ACQUAINTANCE with professional golf consists primarily if not exclusively of the image of a smiling golfer accepting an oversize check from the tournament sponsor on the eighteenth green following his Sunday-afternoon victory ought to visit a tournament site on Monday morning of a tournament week. Here is the feeling of an airport transplanted to the out-of-doors, a conglomeration of people coming and going many ways, and for all of them, even the traffic guards, there is a sense of anticipation, because the tournament has not yet begun, an anticipation that for the competitors is a weekly rite, renewing hope.

How're you hitting them?

Great, man, great.

There beyond the Harbour Town clubhouse, on the driving range wedged between the ninth green and the tenth tee, several of the early tournament arrivals were already hitting balls. A few of their colleagues, including a former U.S. Open champion, Hubert Green, were already on the course. In fact, Hubert was on the seventeenth, a nifty par three that faces the water and brings players into the open sea air of Calibogue Sound, the spectacular setting of the eighteenth, the course's signature hole, with a view of Harbour Town's lighthouse in the distance behind the eighteenth green.

Hubert Green was practicing for the tournament by himself. Forty-six years old, he had been playing on the tour since turning professional in 1970. He had won nineteen tour events, including this one, the MCI Heritage Classic, back in 1976 when it was just called the Sea Pines Heritage Classic. Back then, Green was one of the top golfers on the tour, but his star had slipped since his last tour victory, a major, the 1985 PGA Championship. Now the ten-year exemption he had earned with that victory was about to run out. The previous year he had entered nineteen tournaments and made the cut in only four. His earnings were a paltry $18,031, not even enough to pay his expenses on the road. His ranking for the year had been 212th.

Once someone playing in a pro-am with Green reputedly asked Green how he was, and the intense Green, focused on his game, which was already in decline, had reportedly shot back that he was a former U.S. Open champion and who was this person asking *him* how he felt? It was not clear if the possibly apocryphal story was a reflection on Green or on the person who told it. Now, Green hit four practice tee shots at seventeen, three of which landed in a bunker. This was not a good time to bother him. Perhaps he was just trying to keep his game sharp until he was old enough to play on the Senior Tour. Or perhaps he still thought he could win, if not the tournament itself than at least the mini pro-am event in which he was scheduled to participate shortly. In fact, he was going to be late for his twelve-eighteen tee time if he didn't hurry.

Certainly the allure of Mondays, the thought that runs through the minds of most of the players, young and old, is the belief that finally and incontrovertibly, *this* is going to be *the week*. The game does this to people. Unlike other sports, where once you achieve a certain level of competence you can be expected to perform at a reasonable level of proficiency for a certain indefinable but nevertheless predictable period of time, golf even at its highest levels is a game in which the very best players sometimes feel completely out of sorts, just as even the most journeyman of entrants in a given tournament may go on to shoot a record score. It is extremely confounding, and also a main source of the game's appeal to players at every level.

14. Down the Fairway

THE BEACH IS a short walk from the Days Inn, just across the dark tree-lined street, so at night the lights coming from windows in the hotels and condos along the other side of the street seem beckoning, especially the brighter lights toward the newer area of town called Coligny Plaza, where there is a boardwalk that connects the sidewalk to the beach, where college kids play beach volleyball in the daytime, the well-tanned guys mostly wearing bathing suits cut like boxer shorts and the ladies in bikinis, most of them, though every so often there is one with a thong.

Along the Atlantic coast in many towns they have bylaws prohibiting thongs, or bylaws being considered for adoption. In Palm Beach there are no thongs. In Palm Beach there was a woman who used to wear a thong and no top and she sold hot dogs from a cart at a street corner. So they banned thongs.

You never see thongs at a professional golf tournament as you walk along some well-cut fairway, with the leaves from the many trees at Harbour Town so thick and expansive that they were recently trimmed back because some of the greens had been getting too much shade and there was hardly room to shoot at the pins on some of the holes with certain pin placements. (The overhanging limbs with their leaves were making the fairways very narrow.)

Walking along them this week, the South Carolina April sun on your neck, hot like a summer sun up north, you smelled flowers. Along the fairways stood palatial homes, none of them empty, and everyone walked by them while following a group of golfers on the course, everyone looking tremendously healthy in the sunshine, many of the men wearing shorts and the women in matching pastel shorts and suggestive shirts, as if golf were being watched because it gave shape and purpose to what for some golf fans was a day-long prelude to procreation in paradise.

15. In the Sand

NOT AT ALL chilly on the beach. No one out.

Walking across the beach, toward the water, calm tonight, tide out.

If a person had turned right and walked for several miles he would have come, eventually, to Harbour Town. But what breaks in the beach were there? Did the beach stretch without danger all the way to the golf course?

The beach was wide, with the smell of fairway grass in memory and the sensation of beach grass underfoot, the sound of waves rippling, and the sight of waves and lights, numerous near the Hilton, a quite new-looking, multistoried affair laid out in such a way that, from the perspective of the beach, it seemed all the rooms were somehow pointed at the water. Walking toward those lights, the steps to a narrow boardwalk, really a maze of interconnected boardwalks that kept you from damaging the dune grass, took you, via several routes past pools and outdoor bars, to the back of the Hilton lobby.

16. In Gypsy's Kitchen

THOUGH IT HAD been extremely difficult to find a room at the Days Inn, the Hilton did not seem at all crowded. In fact, it seemed empty. Perhaps it was the hour. What hour was that?

Dinner here was something you'd want someone else to be paying for. On your own tab there was better luck in the lounge, where you could fill yourself with enough happy-hour snack food to ward off stomach pangs. Better yet were recep-

Will this putt win another trophy, or join a list of near-misses more talked about than other players' victories?

Johnny Miller (winning at Pebble Beach in 1994), Lee Trevino (still winning on the Senior Tour), and Tom Watson, three of the last players to dominate professional golf before Greg Norman's arrival on the scene.

The first great might-have-been:
the Shark zeros in on victory
at the 1984 U.S. Open, only to be
bitten by the ultimate winner,
Fuzzy Zoeller.

In the last round of the 1986 Masters,
Norman can't keep out of trouble, and
Jack Nicklaus crowns his legend with
yet another major.

Norman shows how resourceful a shark can be, hitting out of a pot bunker . . .

. . . and going on to win his first major at the 1986 British Open at Turnberry.

Two world-famous icons: the Great White Shark and a Ferrari.

Stalking victory at the 1987 Masters, only to see Larry Mize snatch the trophy from his grasp on the second play-off hole.

Brad Faxon displays his short-game prowess at the 1994 British Open.

Nick Faldo puzzled by the lie, but
determined to get back onto the
major-winning track.

Bernhard Langer, the born-again German who won't let the yips stand in the way of winning, and Fred Couples, as carefree as his back will allow.

Credit: PGA Tour / Sam Greenwood

Lee Janzen, Ernie Els, and Corey Pavin, the last three winners of the U.S. Open: two young Turks and the grittiest guy on Tour.

Credit: ALLSPORT / Gary Newkirk

Credit: PGA Tour / Sam Greenwood

Credit: ALLSPORT / Stephen Dunn

Can Peter Jacobsen extend the success he achieved in 1995, or will he find it as tough to keep winning big as Nick Price did after 1993 and 1994?

Credit: ALLSPORT / Claus Andersen

John Daly displays the unmitigated power, and the attitude, that make him the Roseanne of golf.

Greg Norman, sometimes down but never out, notches another victory at the 1995 NEC World Series of Golf. The Great White Shark is still king of the hill—and now the all-time leading money winner on the PGA Tour.

tions, where the drinks were free, too. Once at another golf tournament, where a mixed drink in the media headquarters hotel was $6.95 plus tax and tip, automatically added in, a sign by an open door that said "PGA Sponsors" welcomed guests into a carpeted room filled with guys who had been playing in that day's pro-am, for which they or their corporate sponsors had ponied up two grand or so per "am." Accepting a glass of champagne proffered by a welcoming waiter, interlopers could then attack the very succulent chicken wings arrayed on a nearby table, for the most part ignored by guys whose sponsors would also be picking up the cost of their dinners. These wings were destined to rank among the finest free food on the road, though the prize probably would always go to the tenderloin in a corporate hospitality tent at the B.C. Open in homey Endicott, New York. Or was the tenderloin served at the SONY Ranking reception, the one where they were giving out those nifty white golf shirts with the little green emblem sewn on, *SONY Ranking,* to commemorate the world golf rankings actually devised not by SONY but by the Cleveland-based agent and producing colossus International Management Group? Not just golfers but golf patrons on the PGA Tour are a pampered, catered lot.

At the Hilton bar called Scarlett's the Atlanta Braves were playing on TBS.

Mary, the bartender, said she was an Atlanta Braves fan.

"I've lived here eleven years," she said. Her husband was a carpenter. She said this while Deion Sanders batted.

Neon Deion. The Shark. Scarlett's.

The other night at TGIF's, there had been a wait for a table and the hostess had told latecomers to eat at the bar. There sat a man named Tom Mascari whose suntan and dress made him seem a golfer, but he was too old to be playing on the regular tour.

"Order the New York strip," Mascari had said to the man next to him.

"Yeah?"

"Yeah," he replied. "Order the fucking New York strip. It's a good steak. Good price.

"So what else do you want to know?" he continued. "You ever go deep-sea fishing? Ever need a boat? Here's my card. 'Sport Fishing. The *Rave*. Tom Mascari, owner.' There's my phone numbers. You can do a day, half day, a week, whatever you want. Just call me.

"But it's just fishing.

"Now then, order the goddam steak.

"What are you drinking? Mine's a Manhattan. A Manhattan, for Chrissakes. Who the fuck even knows what a Manhattan is anymore?

"This one isn't bad."

Mascari had been around earlier, probably at Gypsy's. Gypsy's was a mobile trailer run by Joe Grillo, called Gypsy by everyone, for the benefit of caddies. In the trailer was a small kitchen, and Gypsy traveled from tournament to tournament to cook good food at very low prices for the caddies and anyone else permitted entry. Some of the players had discovered Gypsy's kitchen, and some of them had donated money to Gypsy to keep the enterprise going. Their names, posted on a board outside the trailer, included Greg Norman and Brad Faxon.

Fax, who has known Gypsy for more than ten years, owes part of his professional success to Gypsy, who was his caddy at the Qualifying School tournament he entered in the fall of 1983 in Ponte Vedra, the only Q-School in which he had ever had to play in his entire professional career.

"Just think about golf," Gypsy told Faxon when the pressure had started to build during that tension-filled week a decade ago. "That's why you're here.

"No. Take it back a little slower." This was on the range, where Gypsy had been standing behind Faxon before the final round.

"I'm going to hit this out of a divot, and it's going to draw," Faxon had said.

Assuming his stance, Faxon brought his club back and, sticking his tongue out as he often used to during a swing, sent the ball with the sound of a pistol crack 210 yards to the right, then drawing left.

"I've got some butterflies," he said.

"Good," replied Gypsy. "Me, too."

Of medium height but stocky, with a black mustache that frames a harried smile, Gypsy was a man in perpetual motion while he cooked during tournaments. Before he caddied he had been a chef, and though he still caddied occasionally, as he had for Steve Jones when Jones won the season-opening Tournament of Champions in 1992, he could usually be found in his kitchen trailer rather than on the course since his regular "bag," Jim Simons, had stopped playing the tour regularly in the late 1980s. Sometimes, with the six-figure income that a few of the caddies earn toting the bags of the most famous, financially successful players, Gypsy thought about giving up his cooking, which he started doing because so many of the caddies were not only poor but poorly treated. He started a caddies' association, lobbying for such caddy rights as the use of on-course portable bathrooms sometimes reserved for players only.

The father of several children, one of whom was helping out in the kitchen, Gypsy listed his official home as San Antonio, but he wasn't there much (until he left the tour later amidst allegations of poor financial management).

"Hey, Gypsy, that was a great salad. What you got today for dessert?"

"Yeah, I love you too. How about some of this, sweetheart?" And he grabbed his crotch.

At Scarlett's, snack selections were listed on the small menu card perched atop the bar. Were there really ten jumbo shrimp in the jumbo shrimp cocktail that was listed at $4.95?

"Yes there are," said Mary. "And they're good."

That afternoon, playing in the Harbour Town Pro-Am, Brad Faxon, after one of the men in his pro-am group had pulled out an unheard-of fifteen-wood, had said to himself, "I've got a feeling this is going to be a long afternoon."

He was referring to the projected length of the round, which in many pro-ams could approach six hours. But he hadn't really meant the comment as a complaint; unlike some of the pros, Faxon seems not only resigned to these Wednesday-afternoon affairs that help pay the tournament bill but to enjoy them for what they are, which is often how he appears to approach every other round of golf he plays, or his time off from golf, for that matter.

Lee Janzen, playing in the group in front of Faxon today, had kidded him about the round while they waited at the seventeenth tee, where the golf traffic had been backed up.

"What happened at Augusta, Fax?" Janzen said, with reference to Faxon's pairing with Norman, who was skipping the tournament this week at Harbour Town. "You intimidate Greg?"

Pleased with his wit, Janzen then hit his tee shot and moved on, with Faxon following a few minutes later. But the banter continued through the end of the round, with whoever was standing nearby.

"Calibogue Sound on the left," Faxon intoned at the eighteenth tee, mimicking the heightened tone of a television commentator. "Condos and out of bounds on the right."

Now it was nighttime on Hilton Head, "the second-largest island in the United States on the Atlantic Ocean coast."

Mary said more people would be coming in over the weekend for the tournament.

"Where you staying?" she asked a barfly.

"Days Inn."

"How is it?"

"It's okay. Service was a little slow at breakfast, so I've been walking to Coligny. Went to that place that has the all-you-can-eat buffet."

"How was it?"

"All right, I guess. I ate too much, but I walked it off. But I got tired of watching other golfers, so I went and played some myself. That usually happens to me at these tournaments."

"Where'd you go?"

"First at the place right down the road from Harbour Town. Sea Marsh. I played with a couple of guys from Boston here on vacation. Played pretty well. Then I went over this evening to the Fazio course. They were closing soon, but they gave me a cart and told me I could play until dark. I almost got in eighteen."

"Enjoy the tournament," she said. She was originally from Long Island. Since moving down here she was always having visitors from up north, especially in the winter. That was fine with her.

Gypsy had been at the Fazio course, too. He had been putting on the practice green while waiting for the rest of his foursome. Who was that?

"Couple of caddies and Daniel."

Daniel is one of his sons, who'd been working with Dad since he graduated from high school. He was going to college in the fall, maybe, but right now he was traveling around the country from golf tournament to tournament. In the trailer, where the television was, above the shelf with newspapers and magazines, *Playboy* and *Penthouse,* there were two seats, one for the driver and the other his passenger, and that is where Gypsy and Daniel sat as they drove across America. You didn't see the seats when you came into the trailer for a meal unless you looked for them. What did father and son talk about as they drove? Did Gypsy tell Daniel stories about the tour, about the road, about surviving on the road?

One evening at Gypsy's during a U.S. Open only Daniel was there. The kitchen was closed, but there was coffee. A few caddies were sitting outside the trailer, drinking coffee under the portable awning, some of them smoking cigarettes. The trailer that week had been parked near a practice green, and Daniel was on the green, putter in hand, putting. Nearby, Sandy Lyle, a former British Open champion, was chipping balls from just off the green to one of several practice holes where Daniel was putting. No one talked, no one else watched. Lyle worked on a shot that was a cross between a chip and a putt. Placing ball after ball at the edge of the fringe, where its short grass met the longer grass of the rough, he "putted" with his sand wedge, which enabled him to get the clubhead back without its being impeded by the long grass the way a putter's head would be. Finally Lyle left and only Daniel remained on the green as late afternoon drifted into early evening, the air hot and humid, boisterous voices coming from the open windows of a nearby lounge.

How that incongruous image remained, the trailer parked by the putting green to a country club so exclusive there is a waiting list to get on the waiting list. There is no waiting list to get into Gypsy's kitchen.

17. Lost and Found

BACK ALONG THE boardwalk to the beach, then the boardwalk to Coligny Plaza: shops, ice cream, cut across Pope Avenue, the main road that intersects with South Forest Beach, the road along which the Days Inn is located. A shortcut past TGIF: cross the parking lot by the restaurant, enter an adjacent condominium complex, follow walkway to the back of the Days Inn property, quick swim before going to bed.

"Calibogue Sound on the right. Condos and out of bounds on the left!"

Earlier, sitting in the rear of the small press tent at the edge of the parking lot by the walkway to the Harbour Town clubhouse, a startling greeting from former U.S. Open champion Payne Stewart upon his entrance for a press conference.

"Don't rise," Stewart had joked.

Not a chance, Payne baby. Not a chance.

The semiflamboyant Stewart, perhaps best known because for several years he was paid by the National Football League to wear knickers, shirt, and socks in color schemes that mirror those of NFL teams, followed his 1991 U.S. Open victory with the worst season of his professional golfing career since his rookie year of 1981. He had finished forty-fourth on the money list in 1992.

Perhaps Stewart's rudeness in the press tent wasn't the boast it seemed. Perhaps it was a revelation, however indirect and apparently unconscious, of a state of mind not at all unfamiliar to professional golfers who have lost their way and are not sure which way to go next.

Brad Faxon, after finishing the eighteenth today, bummed a ride on a golf cart back to the clubhouse, because the eighteenth green sat on a little promontory by the water and was a much longer distance from the clubhouse than was typical. Half a mile maybe. A volunteer drove the cart, which had a bench seat. Brad slid in next to the volunteer, with Cubby on the outside. Brad's clubs were in back, in his black Titleist bag. The clubs inside rattled as the cart rode over bumps in the cart path. He passed a trio of young women who recognized Faxon as a pro golfer they had seen playing during the day. Everyone waved, but the cart continued, the breeze made by its motion blowing Faxon's hair. That breeze felt cool after the long hot round in the sun.

This was also the day the tour had announced a settlement in its long dispute with one of the prominent golf club manufacturers, Karsten Manufacturing Corporation, makers of Ping, over the tournament use of clubs with so-called square grooves. Because he was an elected player representative on the tour's policy board, Brad had been summoned during the pro-am round to read a draft of the press release that was being distributed as he arrived at the clubhouse. Instead of practicing this afternoon, or having fun with his kids, Brad had to attend further meetings about the issue, while Bonnie Faxon in the courtesy Cadillac they were driving this week took Cubby back to the rented house where his wife, Shelley, was waiting for him.

Now, at the end of what by the sign was Cordillo Parkway, which indeed intersected with Forest Beach, a turn then onto Forest Beach, and it was not long before ahead were condos and ocean on the right, air-conditioned patio room (pool view, twin double beds, free cable, Touch-Tone phones), home on the road safe harbor Days Inn on the left.

18. *Playing Your Own Game*

THE FATHER OF a Massachusetts professor once owned a third share of an island south of Hilton Head. Attractive to paper mills, the island was assessed and put up for sale in the early 1970s. The professor's father's share was valued at $10 million, of which the son would receive one-ninth.

"Then the Arab oil embargo began, the economy went slack, and my daddy couldn't sell the land. Eventually the state bought it and made a park."

The professor, a pipe-smoking, nongolfing, tennis-playing psychologist, was not bitter. But with the park any dream of his becoming rich died like the light of the fireflies on this warm night, or a golf ball dropping out of sight into the salt marsh fronting the green on the last hole at Harbour Town.

They say in golf you have to play your own game: find out what that game is and then stick with it. Doing so is harder than it may sound, for a golfer is always tempted to try a new shot, experiment with a new approach, and invariably ends up paying for it. If your game is a short one and you generally post your best scores when you lay the ball up on the par fours and then get down in two with a chip and putt—if that's your game, then you have to play it, even when your opponent is hitting by you from the tee.

Nick Price, whose 1993 Players Championship victory was one of several that would propel him, eventually, to making a run at being the dominant player in the world, liked to say you had to find your own pace.

"Yeah," Nick said, after that victory. "I saw Greg's shot on seventeen. That was a relief. But then I was disappointed for him, because he had just birdied fifteen and sixteen.

"The pressure was unbelievable this week. I didn't want to go to sleep with the lead. These were the longest four days, sleeping on the lead.

"You think about the small things, that will take care of the big things. When you're playing well, you don't see the trouble.

"Last year at Augusta I had great ball-striking. So it was wearing when I didn't make any putts.

"I'm grateful to my wife for many years of persevering. I've played five hundred tournaments and just started winning. There's a difference between having it in you and doing it."

EACH GOLFER IS different, according to Price; each golfer's pace is also different.

"It's a simple philosophy I have," he told me. "You really only feel you have a chance to win when you have a certain amount of control. It's hard to put that in a percentage or out-of-ten scale, but you feel like your game is coming together, the ball is reacting off the clubface the way your brain is telling it it should, so if you hit the shot and say, 'Well, I cut that one,' your feelings are correct.

"To win in golf you have to be in control of so many things. Your long game or driving game. Your iron game. Your short game. Bunker play. And your putting. And you have to be disciplined enough to control your mind from wandering away from what you are trying to do, which is something that happens quite frequently. You might be out there dreaming about something else when you should be thinking about the next shot. Also, you have to control your emotions, trying not to get too excited when you play well, or when you're depressed and playing poorly you might want to bang your club but you know that's not good for your score. There are a lot of controlling factors.

"I don't like to use the word fear. It's something that shouldn't even factor into it. If you can use your nervous energy, channel it in the right direction by controlling your emotions—if you can control your emotions in your pre-shot routine really well, then you channel that nervous energy through your shot. That's when I hit shots that quite astound me sometimes.

"What is being nervous? Nervous is being unsure, but fear is not being able to do anything. If you don't have nervousness you're not going to be able to play to the best of your ability. Those nerves, those butterflies, heighten your senses and make your brain work just that little bit better, little bit clearer.

"There is also fear of success: getting into the unknown. What's going to happen if you do this?

"What kicks in for me is that golf is something I've always wanted to do, so I want to do the very best I can in golf. Whatever the consequences are, I'm prepared to accept, because I really want this—what I'm doing—to happen. I've practiced so many years of my life to play golf at a standard that I'm now playing that it's very exciting. That's what makes me feel that I can get up and fight the next day."

SHARKBITE

WHEN YOU PUT a lot of energy into any profession, whether it's golf or whatever, you can get tired of it. You can want to walk away from it. You need to walk away from it. You can't indulge yourself in any business a hundred and one percent or you'll burn yourself out very quickly. You have to know when to walk away.

Some people might be different than others. If you learn to understand your own mechanics inside yourself, then you can walk away after two weeks, say I need a rest, or you can stay out there for five weeks. That's just up to the individual. You can't immerse yourself that much into anything without getting away from it. That's why a lot of guys when they get to a position of success in a lot of sports or business can't handle that side of it.

THERE ARE A MILLION advisers out there in this world. I get fan mail daily and there's always somebody out there trying to advise you to do something. I think it's wonderful because they take interest and are concerned about your livelihood. But, at the end of the day, you're the one who's got to decide which are the best ways.

STALKING THE SHARK

LONG BEFORE I left the tour in Rochester, I had learned there was an intimate connection between playing golf for a living and playing and watching it for fun.

Like Greg Norman and 25 million other men and women in the United States, give or take a few hundred thousand, I play golf. And like seventy-six-year-old Dr. Artie Lepine, I think about golf when I'm not playing. Semiretired as a dentist, Dr. Artie Lepine also plays golf every day.

"But only eighteen holes," he sighs. "I used to get in twenty-seven, sometimes forty-five a day. Actually I've played as many as fifty-four holes of golf in one day."

He has also scored an astounding eleven holes in one, including three at the same hole within a glorious six-week period.

When Lepine was still practicing dentistry full-time, he once left the office for an important golf match without remembering that one of the chairs in his office still had a patient in it.

"They called me when I got to the course," Lepine confesses. "I told them to dismiss the patient."

Now a member at two golf courses, Lepine in the past belonged also to two others. That was in the days when he carried a six handicap, a figure that has risen lately to twenty-seven.

"I can't hit the ball the way I used to," Lepine laments. But he hardly sounds sorry for himself.

For one thing, there are the matches he plays with his son Todd, a doctor who lives about an hour's drive from his father. The two men get along so well, and Lepine thinks his son's club is such a nice place to play, that he has become an out-of-town member there.

And he loves to tell stories about the simple companionship and good times he has enjoyed on the course.

"I remember one day waiting to hit and a guy behind me hit first and struck me in the rear. We looked for his ball, but we couldn't find it until the next hole, when I reached into my pocket for a coin to use as a marker. The other guy's golf ball, the one that had hit me, was in my pocket!"

Even at the height of his golfing prowess, when he was regularly shooting scores in the high 70s, Artie Lepine never entertained dreams of being a professional golfer.

"I was never *that* good," he says. Pressed, he has difficulty defining how good *that* was.

A pro golfer, he believes, must have a certain requisite ability, and then he applies himself. It is not unlike becoming a brain surgeon, Dr. Lepine concludes upon reflection, because you really have to be *highly qualified.*

"And I wasn't," he admits cheerfully. And then wistfully adds, "Oh, but I had some unbelievable shots."

When he isn't playing golf, Dr. Lepine likes to watch it on television. He says he follows the big guys.

"Couples. That Price guy.

"And, oh yes, the Shark."

I REMEMBER A summer night after I had been playing golf when somewhere overhead in the darkening mist the moon was shining so brightly that the sky was lighter than it normally would have been at nine o'clock. I was drenched with sweat, and the mosquitoes were out by the practice tee, where I had put down my golf bag.

A small dark shape flew nearby. A bat.

Setting myself over the ball, I began my swing with my turn, the seven-iron in my hands feeling light, and at the top of my backswing I started moving my hips forward before turning them as I brought my right elbow toward my right hip. When the club returned to the ball the impact was square and flush, and the ball, sailing out over the shadowy fairway, rose into the moonlit haze and hovered over the course, the entire sweet-smelling languorous landscape, as if it were beckoning me to follow in its lovely thrilling flight.

"There's something almost addictive about golf," Greg Norman once told me. "It's a challenge. Golf is one of those few sports, outside of snooker or billiards, where you hit a stationary object from a stationary position. Every other sport, you're on the move with a moving object. And that is the beauty of the game. That's where you get the feeling of, 'God, it looks so simple, but it's so complicated.' "

When my infatuation with golf led me inevitably to the men's pro tour, which I had been watching from afar on television, I began attending tournaments, including a six-day event that served as a qualifier for the tour. The more I saw, the more I wanted to see. How often, watching golf tournaments, did I discover the lazy, addictive pleasure of observing an event that had no gainful purpose, no utilitarian *raison d'être* in the gross national product. The placid, satisfied feeling of calm, not unlike the spentness after sex, could creep over a golfer, too, mid-round, after some especially spectacular accomplishment: the sinking of a long putt, a crisply hit long iron to a distant green, an explosion shot out of a bunker that stopped a foot from the pin. That sense of being on top of things, of being in control, of knowing where you are and why, can be terribly fleeting.

And extraordinarily exhilarating.

Even the pros, I discovered, could become animated when they saw someone else hit a great shot. After Raymond Floyd won the 1993 Shark Shootout by sticking a wedge to five feet on the eighteenth at Sherwood Oaks, Brad Faxon said, wide-eyed, "Whatever you're writing about, Floyd's got it."

Improvising from the tour's own itinerary, I made up my schedule as I went, just as the pros themselves do (none play in all the tournaments). Though they don't officially have to commit their participation in a tournament until Friday after-noon of the week before, I usually planned a little farther ahead than that. I never knew from tournament to tournament what I would find, but I was certain I would recognize a discovery when I encountered it.

Someone has calculated that in a typical four-hour round of golf, the actual elapsed time of golf action (defined as time spent hitting the ball) is between three and four minutes (the range represents the difference between a good player, who takes fewer shots, and an average one, with a further incre-mental difference to account for such variables as backswing speeds). Watching golf on tour, I sometimes felt that law was at work. One fall weekend I drove all the way from my Mass-achusetts home to Endicott, New York, to see some of the B.C. Open. There I dutifully recorded the rounds of several com-petitors, including Brad Faxon and Patrick Burke, neither of whom played particularly well.

Endicott is located in the Leatherstocking region of New York State, not far from Cooperstown. A large sign, which also advertised Michelob beer, said "Welcome PGA Tour and Fans." Endicott is a town where the mail in the public mail-boxes along Main Street is picked up only once a day. There are three nudist colonies in the area. Main Street has four lanes, two of which were being used for parking. Small faded flags hung from lightposts along the street, which is fronted by tidy homes. This, another sign proclaimed, was the "Home of the

Square Deal." As you walked through town, you heard the whistle of the train, and all around was the bustle and atmosphere of a small country fair. The driving range used by the players during the B.C. Open was really a *range,* a mile or so down a side road from the En-Joie course. To reach it, the players had to be driven in minivans. There was a palpable sense here in late September of a summer just past, the air in the park-like tree-lined fairways smelling of early autumn, the traffic hum coming from just off Main Street sounding busy. A sewage treatment plant was located adjacent to a section of the course, and you could smell that, too.

Alex Alexander, the saintly tournament founder and chairman, lived so close to the course where the B.C. Open was played that you could see his house from certain vantage points. He stood at one point by a practice green and thanked the players for coming to the tournament as they passed by him.

Though some of the tour's better players participated because they liked Alexander, this was the kind of tournament that drew a large portion of its field from the pool of players who for one reason or another did not usually get to play in the more prestigious events. There was a corps group of such men, known as grinders, who played wherever they could, as often as they could, sometimes entering nearly three dozen official tournaments a year, just to have a chance to make enough money to be exempt the following season. These players included such people as stocky, quiet Ed Dougherty, who until recently had spent much of his career as a club pro in Pennsylvania before coming back out on tour in his forties. Nearly two years would pass before Dougherty, at the age of forty-seven and with time running out in his career, would win his first PGA Tour event in 1995.

"That's about as emotional as I've ever been on the course," he would say. "At the eighteenth, I knew the tournament wasn't over. When I heard the people applaud, it was so special. They've always been clapping for someone else."

ON SATURDAY OF the 1993 B.C. Open, a veteran, Buddy Gardner, was having breakfast at Gypsy's. Gypsy greeted Buddy as an old-timer.

"Yeah," said Buddy. "Old as you are."

An hour before the first tee time on Saturday, volunteer workers were still arriving. "We do everything," said one.

Over on the range, the players who had made the cut were warming up. Caddies with towels dried off the clubs, carefully wiping the handles. Because players had different tee times, those on the range were in different stages of their warm-ups, which meant that one player was hitting balls with his driver, while the one next to him might be making short shots with his sand wedge. After a player was done, a volunteer from the range shop picked up any balls that had been left near the place where the player had been swinging and took them back to the shop in a metal range basket. It was so wet that Larry Mize's caddy was wearing rubbers over his new Reeboks.

Brad Faxon arrived at eight-thirty and stayed only fifteen or twenty minutes. He would not be playing in the next week's tournament, so Cubby was going to work for Gary Halberg. Faxon's warm-up here might have been the shortest of anyone's, but he had little chance of making a big check this week and seemed to be going through the motions. Golfers sometimes play especially well when they are in such a situation. The day before, as soon as he said he'd had it, Faxon made several birdies.

Joey Sindelar, who grew up near here, had won this tournament twice, but he couldn't play in the 1993 event because he had injured his hand. Among the competitors was Brett Ogle, who had made a name for himself as the winner of that year's Pebble Beach tournament. Ogle, one of only two tour players to regularly use a long putter (Bruce Leitzke was the other), was something of a free spirit, at least by tour standards. Ogle liked to wear wraparound sunglasses when he played, and he snuck an occasional cigarette during tournament play.

Golf action at the B.C. Open, except when it involved the leaders, was apt to take place in front of extremely small crowds. Even good players, if they were not in contention, played in almost total obscurity, save for the holes that ran along the clubhouse area, where some fans positioned themselves for the day and didn't move. Brad Faxon, who probably would have been playing in the Ryder Club the week of the '93 B.C. Open if he had not had his skiing accident the previous winter, framed some so-so golf around some spectacular shots, such as a nice wedge to six feet on the par-four twelfth, but there was almost no one there to watch. Away from the TV cameras (until the advent of the Golf Channel, there was no television coverage of the B.C. Open) and away from the leader board, this was typical of how much professional golf is played. Even at the big tournaments, there are usually very small crowds early in the week during practice days, and, unless it is a high profile event, the Wednesday pro-am. Once a tournament begins, the majority of players typically play before a gallery consisting of a few family members and friends with the occasional interloper.

PLAYING BEHIND FAXON on Friday at the B.C. Open, Patrick Burke at one point was two under. On the twelfth, he hit a four-wood 246 yards and missed the eagle putt. Then he missed the birdie putt. On the thirteenth, his approach shot landed just short of the green, so he had to putt it from the fringe, where according to the rules he was not permitted to clean the ball, which had some mud on it.

"Shit on you, ball," said Burke.

Play had slowed as he moved to the next tee, where he said,

"Is it going to rain? If I'm leading, I'll hire some planes to make it rain." He meant that if he was the leader at the halfway point and the tournament was called off because of rain, he would be declared the winner because he was ahead after the first two rounds.

Burke's playing partner said on the fifteenth, "If I birdie this one, I'll buy everyone a drink." Responded Burke: "If I birdie the hole, he'll buy you a drink."

Farther behind them, the actual leader, Jim McGovern, had dropped to minus eight. A fan who had been following Mc-Govern seemed unfamiliar with the putting-green routine.

"Joe, you got to stand still," said a caddy to the fan. The fan looked confused. He stood in the line of the putt.

"Joe, now you got to move," said the caddy with annoyance.

After McGovern two-putted, he tossed the ball to "Joe." "Here," he said, shaking his head. "A souvenir."

THERE WAS A tradition at the B.C. Open, a dinner for the caddies put on in a pavilion by the course by the tournament host. The caddy dinner menu was chicken, salad, rolls, and beer. The caddies sat at long tables and ate in small groups. At the far end of the room from the food, new sunglasses were given out to any caddy who was a member of the caddy association started by Gypsy. A caddy named Dow, who said he was from Dallas, reported he had been away from home thirty-two weeks that year. "I've made eighteen thousand," he said. The average player would probably have gone through at least three times that amount just to cover his expenses. Here at Endicott, caddies could save a little, because in addition to this free dinner, hotel rooms were so cheap. (The most expensive places to caddy are the resorts like Hilton Head, where the caddies sometimes live four to a room.)

The next night the so-called caddies' hockey game was held at a rink called the Polar Cap, about half an hour away. Very few caddies came, though one who did, Cubby Burke, was a standout because he still coached a semipro hockey team in Sun Valley, Idaho, in the winter. An immense presence on the ice, wearing sweatpants with shin guards underneath, Cubby lined up his employer, Brad Faxon, for a check that he never gave.

"Man!" he exclaimed afterward. "I could have fucking nailed him!"

One of two pro golfers to play in the pickup game, which also included a former New York Ranger, Pierre Laganiere, Faxon skated with an enthusiasm that compensated for his rustiness. He wore the pants and uniform shirt of the Hartford Whalers. Faster and smoother was Patrick Burke, who said, "I'd trade fifteen fucking years on the golf tour for ten fucking years playing pro hockey."

The unheated rink was empty save for the players and one observer, pro golfer Rick Fehr. After two hours of ice time, everyone gathered in the rink's refreshment lounge, which served beer. The year before, Patrick Burke confessed, he had stayed out after the game until three o'clock and the next morning arrived at the course without time for warming up.

"I hit the worst shot I've ever seen a pro hit," he boasted.

This night ended earlier, but not before Burke remembered when he had been paired with Faxon in a tournament. "I hit the ball farther," he said. "And straighter."

"But I lost by two strokes."

Outside the Polar Cap, hard by the Chenango River, it was dark and chilly. Downtown Binghamton, on the way back to Endicott, was deserted and dilapidated, the art-deco front of the Greyhound building faded, the brick of the old Lackawanna Railroad station burnt orange. There were no trains that came through this once thriving passenger center, a major stop to and from New York City. The station now housed the Southern Tier Academy of Dance and Gymnastics.

A weather front was moving in, and it began raining the next morning, shortly after the first groups of golfers had started.

Play was suspended for a time, and some of the players gathered in Gypsy's kitchen trailer, drinking coffee and watching the Ryder Cup matches from England on television. There was loud cheering for the American side and derision when the camera focused on Nick Faldo's shocked facial expression upon missing a putt. Before I left I asked Gypsy if he was going to be needing a caddy in the caddies' golf tournament, held here the day after the tournament.

"No thanks, man. I like to ride."

I HAD KNOWN from the start of my golf watching that despite whatever I saw there was always going to be another tournament I had missed. This gave my journeys a kind of quixotic shape, which seemed in keeping with my subject. Even such a compulsively organized man as Greg Norman still has no idea what will happen to him during a given week on tour.

I followed the tour from my backyard, where I chip orange-colored plastic golf balls with holes in them into a conical net suspended on an aluminum frame, to Florida, where the tour spends the entire month of March. I followed it to Georgia and South Carolina, to New Jersey and New York, to Connecticut and back to Massachusetts. I crossed the country several times to watch professional golf in such places as Portland, Oregon, and Pebble Beach, California.

I took with me some advice I received from my golfing friend, Paul Venne, who would celebrate his ninetieth birthday in 1996. After his retirement from the tire business almost a quarter of a century ago, Venne moved to western Massachusetts, where his wife had grown up. He joined the nine-hole course in Amherst owned by Amherst College and began helping out in the pro shop. Eventually arthritis curtailed his golf, and most of his free time was devoted to taking care of his ailing wife. But he still came into the club every weekday morning to open up and make coffee.

And to talk about golf.

Unlike the conversation of more active golfers, however, Venne's golf talk tended to veer away from the mysteries of the swing and toward the idiosyncrasies of friends, many of whom were no longer living. One morning, talking about the money professional golfers make and, in many cases, seem to regard as their entitlement, Venne laughed about two relatives who he said were millionaires.

"They are no happier than I," he said.

Clean shaven, neatly dressed, and wearing a white cap on his head, Venne wouldn't let me pay for my coffee.

"I give away all the money I can," he said. "Last month I had an extra $1,200 in my checking account. I gave it to my son. My father used to give away money, too. What do I need it for?"

Thinking about Paul Venne, I followed the tour to Augusta, where two months before I had called the club to apply for a media badge, initially citing my affiliation with a general-interest magazine. The press secretary, Martha Gay, imperiously explained that only writers for accredited sports magazines need apply. The club received far more requests than it could handle.

"I just turned down *Forbes*," Mrs. Gay boasted. "I wouldn't really care if you were calling on behalf of *Newsweek.*"

I then said I was planning to write a book. Evidently this barred me from any further consideration, because Mrs. Gay announced triumphantly that a book was not a publication. Though I pleaded my case further with what I thought was extreme logic and the kind of courtesy I falsely imagined was valued at such a genteel place, Mrs. Gay was not going to be dissuaded.

A friend, hearing later what had occurred between Mrs. Gay and me, and knowing that I planned to attend the tournament following the Masters, the MCI Heritage Classic at Hilton Head, South Carolina, urged me to leave for that tournament a day early.

"Drive up to Augusta on Sunday," he said. "You'll get in." He was right.

But even before I reached Augusta my perception of the place had been altered by the kind of chance encounter that can bedevil or bewitch anyone living on the road, whether he is a golf player or a golf writer.

Arriving the night before at the Savannah, Georgia, airport, I had gone to the Hertz counter to pick up a rental car I had reserved. The clerk said there was an overstock of certain vehicles and for only a few dollars more a day how would I like a brand-new, fire-engine-red, eight-cylinder Thunderbird?

Why not?

Driving to Augusta the next morning, I took what appeared on the map to be the most direct route. Instead of following an interstate west and then another north, I opted for state highways that went more or less in a straight line northwest. There wouldn't be much traffic at this hour, and maybe I'd see something along the way. Something such as a peach farm or an old schoolhouse by a four corners or a quiet Main Street in a quiet Georgia town, the kind of scene that televised golf shows are forever incorporating as background, as if to imply that golf only takes place in a Norman Rockwell context. Though I knew those representations were false, I imagined myself this morning driving into a golf telecast.

"Shit," I said to myself as I saw the blinking red light in my rearview mirror, just after I heard the siren. I'd hardly been touching the accelerator in my T-bird, but I noticed before I slowed down that I had been going eighty-two miles per hour. I wasn't sure what the speed limit was, but I imagined it was no more than fifty.

I was right.

"Y'all going to church?"

"No, sir," I replied. Even now, early on this beautiful spring morning in Georgia, the sky clear and the sun already warming the air into the seventies, I felt a little better under the circumstances I was in conversing in formal salutations. It was like the vicarious thrill a nonmilitary person gets when giving or receiving a salute. "No, sir. I'm not going to church. I'm going to the golf tournament in Augusta. The Masters."

Revealing that destination sealed my fate. Whatever naiveté had prompted me to think all Georgians were golf fanatics during Masters week was quickly erased by the frown on the officer's brow.

"Is that right," said the officer, forgetting to call me sir. "The Masters. Let's have a look at your driver's license."

Then he disappeared into his cruiser for what seemed a long time. I waited nervously for his return. Perhaps he would give me a warning rather than a ticket.

"Sir."

I knew what was coming. But where was my license? He had evidently anticipated this question.

"We have a special program here for our out-of-state visitors," he explained. "We goin' to hold your driver's license until we receive payment for the citation." The citation, he continued, was also a temporary license, good for twenty-one days. In a legal sense, I was posting bail with my license, which I would recover upon payment of my $50 fine.

I was about to inquire about the consequences of my being stopped again by another policeman and having to produce the citation as my "license," but an inner voice saved me from the destiny such a question would surely have sealed. I drove on, anxious in my anticipation of the event for which I still had no ticket, my pulse racing a little as it does for any golfer on the first tee before a match.

Nervous now that I was in Augusta, because I feared my trip might be in vain, I looked for a bank with an ATM along the capacious highway strip, eerily quiet because the stores were closed on this Easter Sunday. I finally found one after driving in a circle for fifteen more minutes. Then, in the confusing street system around the outside of Augusta, I had to get to the course, which lay on the other side of the city from where I had come in.

Here I was, on a glorious April morning, no more than two or three miles from my destination, and I kept going around it. I tried to remain calm. I played some music I had brought with me on the T-bird's tape deck. When at last I made the correct turn onto Washington Road and could tell from the way the traffic was backed up that I was getting close, I started worrying again about getting in.

And dreaming about what I would see if I did, dreaming about the holes on the back nine named Amen Corner by former *New Yorker* golf writer Herbert Warren Wind, whose elegant essays about golf tournaments often began with several-thousand-word leads. Wind, I recalled, never seemed anxious in his work, nor did his golfers. Perhaps times had changed.

I was directed to the large lot of a shopping plaza. All my travel belongings, of course, were in the trunk of the T-bird, which would easily reach a temperature of over a hundred degrees by midday. There was nothing I could do but leave everything. I had remembered a hat, which I wore, and sunblock, which I used before I locked the car. In my wallet were ten new $20 bills, several of which would shortly be in the possession of a scalper on Washington Road.

The next year, after failing again not only with Mrs. Gay but with one of the stalwarts of the club, a man who had golfed with founder Bobby Jones, I once more tried my friend, who this time secured an actual badge for me through a member. We met at the club, where I asked him if I owed him anything, and he replied he would take a check for $100, the face value of the badge, which prior to the tournament was commanding a street price in the thousands.

MY VISITS TO the Masters confirmed a feeling I had entertained since I began watching golf up close, that the tour was one continuous tournament. Arriving in Jacksonville for the Players Championship, I walked through the cool JAX terminal with its tasteful souvenir stands that in comparison to the usual airport fare seem like boutiques at a tony mall. Outside, with that first rush of hot air, sucking it in, great gulps of Florida sunshine air, I looked for a ride to the Jacksonville Beach Comfort Inn (Oceanfront). Turning to the nearest nontourist in his Bermudas, near a group of business executives who must have been on their way to the Amelia Island Conference Center, where they would finally shed their suits and in the programmed afternoons steal outside to use the golf bags now lined up like foot soldiers at their sides, I asked, "What's that . . . fragrance?" and a man in shorts answered, "Paper mill."

The next night, I put down my newspaper and walked outside into the warm, vast vista of lawn and asphalt and small buildings that defines northern Florida. Outside, the nighttime breeze made goose bumps on my bare arms, below the sleeves of the green-and-white-striped Izod sweatshirt that was my gift from the PGA Tour for covering the TPC this week.

I had nothing particular to do, so I stayed at the course, watching television in the clubhouse bar, browsing in the pro shop, where you could buy every conceivable kind of merchandise with the tournament logo printed on it. You could buy a Players Championship towel that attached to your golf bag for $16. Or a TPC money clip for $15, which was also the price of a TPC brandy snifter. But not a repeating swing.

I scrounged in the media eating area, downstairs next to the media room, which during the rest of the year was the storage area for the course's golf carts. I had spent too much on dinner the night before and I thought I might find a leftover sandwich. While I ate it and drank a Diet Coke I watched CNN, then looked a last time in the media room for any handouts I might have missed.

Though many of the reporters do not drink, and very few of them smoke, there is nevertheless among them a symbolically reassuring attachment to the mores of the past. Back when the AT&T National Pro-Am was still called the Bing Crosby, writers would gather much of their material over drinks in the bar of the Lodge at Pebble Beach. And everyone, it seemed—including the athletes—had a cigarette in his mouth. Now, in an era when most of the golfers visit a fitness trailer that follows them to each tour stop—even Fuzzy Zoeller needs help with his chronically poor back—the media try to follow suit. Hardly anyone smokes. A few free hours on tour for a reporter are apt to be filled with a round of golf, not a round of drinks.

After playing and hitting balls on the range, a typical player goes out to dinner with his wife, perhaps goes shopping or sightseeing, then goes back to the hotel to sleep. Unmarried players or players simply traveling alone live much the same routine. You do not last long on the tour if you stay out late at night. Drug use is very rare. Fewer and fewer of the players drink, especially among the younger ones, who as a group are health nuts. Scandal out here is a man losing his temper over a bad shot.

Months later, stalking the Shark on the first fairway in Westchester, New York, I happened on a fan holding a cellular phone making real estate deals, which reminded me of the time at another tournament when I overheard a man, also holding a cellular phone, holler to the woman with him: "Let's go, sweetheart, I've got a four-o'clock flight to Hong Kong." By then, I had participated in a conference-call interview with 1993 Masters champion Bernhard Langer, who described the game he played so well as "very humbling. I think I *have* it and then I don't have it, which shows we're not in control. Life in general is like that. There is no such thing as security." Perhaps that wisdom partially explained some of John Daly's strange behavior, such as the practice drives I saw him hit at the Greater Hartford Open, one after another landing on the roof of the tent beyond the range (with the crowd encouraging him on).

Before I left San Francisco for the first time, I watched Payne Stewart make a backhand motion with his hand to dismiss a marshal who was apparently in Payne's view when he turned his head. The range marshals couldn't keep V. J. Singh supplied with enough practice balls there. "We finally had to throw him off the range," a marshal joked. "He must have practiced five hours."

One night, flying west to stalk the Shark at another tournament, I saw a nearly full moon making visible the snow-capped tops of the Sierra Nevada. The next morning, when Davis Love III arrived at the practice range to warm up, his clubs were already waiting for him. Another player, David Edwards, carried his own to the range. Fans had been arriving since seven-thirty, an hour and a half before the first tee time. Later, on the seventh hole, I watched a Mexican-American member of the grounds crew waiting with a leaf blower to clean the green. After the round a truck drove to all the portable toilets and emptied their contents. And back on the range, Butch Harmon in pink shirt watched his star pupil, the Shark, warm up. When the Shark left the range, fans clapped. When he made a bad shot the next day on the third hole, Butch said, "He'll have no trouble putting it behind him."

The Shark's clear-headed ability to focus on his golf swing, without sentiment, would eventually change his relationship with Harmon. By mid-1995, Greg would also be working with 1993 U.S. Open champion Lee Janzen's teacher, Rick Smith.

At the far end of the range another morning, before they went on the air on Sunday, player and then ABC broadcaster Peter Jacobsen and fellow broadcaster and former LPGA golfer Judy Rankin hit balls. Jacobsen was giving Rankin a lesson. "It doesn't matter what happens before impact," he told her, contradicting much of the accepted wisdom of the golf swing. "What matters is what happens *at* impact."

Before giving up his temporary broadcast post to return to playing full-time, Jacobsen's standard excuse whenever someone needed him for something he didn't want to do was "I've got a production meeting." Inside the ABC broadcast booth above the eighteenth one day, discussion focused on a poor shot by Rick Fehr. Said Jacobsen to anchor Brent Musburger:

"Ask me if that shot was a good play." He meant: "Ask me when we're on camera."

Hitting balls with Rankin, Jacobsen said, was "the highlight of our day. Now we have to go watch other people do it. That's like watching *those* movies at the hotel on Spectravision."

Though I had just traveled three thousand miles to watch the same people play golf that Jacobsen was talking about, I did not feel let down by his remark. By then, I think, I had already started to realize that I was on a journey whose destination I might never reach. The more I stalked the Shark, the less I felt I knew who he was. Each time I saw him play, I was less certain what had really happened to him at the Olympic Club. He had lost a golf tournament. Analysis was elusive at best and inaccurate at worst. It was like the search for the perfect swing.

"Actually," Butch Harmon said to me after I had complimented a round we had just seen Norman watch—"actually, he played better yesterday. But he putted like a dog."

ONE DAY IN June I found Brad Faxon on the putting green of the Westchester Country Club. We had known each other almost ten years, since I had followed him around during the final rounds of the 1983 PGA Tour Qualifying School, the event that enabled him to join the tour as a regular player. He had just graduated from Furman University then, where he won the 1983 Fred Haskins Award as the best collegiate player in the country. Over the summer after his graduation he had played in a few professional events, including the U.S. Open at Oakmont, in which he finished as the top amateur (that was already his third U.S. Open, his first coming after his sophomore year in college). He turned pro right after that tournament, but he couldn't compete regularly until he had successfully made it through Q-School, the six-round torture test that the majority of professional golfers fail in their first attempt.

I can still remember sitting with Brad in the clubhouse at the Tournament Players Club in Sawgrass, where the 1983

Q-School was held in late November, before Thanksgiving. He had just completed his final round, in which he had been paired with veteran Bob Smith and Paul Azinger, and there was no question his score was going to hold up. Over a beer he reviewed his round, before making phone calls to his friends and family to celebrate this defining moment in his young life.

Even at the age of twenty-two, Faxon already had the poise and self-assurance of a man much older and more accomplished than he. With his reddish-blond hair atop a freckled face whose most prominent feature is its nose, Faxon was not handsome in the striking way some athletes are. But he exuded a sense that he knew who he was. There was nothing he would rather do than play golf, and now he was going to be able to play for a living.

But it would be a very precarious livelihood for several years to come. Never a long hitter, he quickly developed his reputation for being somewhat wild off the tee as well, a shortcoming for which he compensated with his superb short game. That kept him on tour. His personal life was as steady as his rise to prominence. After he married his college sweetheart they settled in Orlando, Florida, a popular address on tour because of the climate that permits year-round practice, its proximity to several tournament sites, and the excellent airport.

After our first meeting in Ponte Vedra, we stayed in touch. I visited him in Rhode Island, where he had grown up, and saw him at tournaments in New England, the New England Classic in Worcester and the Greater Hartford Open. During one visit he gave my son a putting lesson. Another time he autographed a PGA Tour trading card for my mother. I took him and Bonnie out to dinner in Connecticut. We never talked about deeply personal matters, but he was open in conversation and always curious about what I was doing. Tracking Fax's progress on tour became a vicarious pleasure for me. Almost every week I looked up his scores, and eventually I caught up with him in person—this June day on the usually private grounds of the Westchester Country Club outside New York.

Not far from the Hutchinson Parkway, the club is an enclave, a "neighborhood" of huge old homes, many of them built of stone. The clubhouse itself, eight stories tall and built of brick and stucco, serves also as a hotel for guests. And there are sixty housekeeping apartments. This helps give the place the feel of another era, when golf was still the domain of the privileged, and a professional golfer was apt to be a gambler. The pro tour takes over Westchester one week each year, for a tournament currently called the Buick Classic, one of four PGA Tour events sponsored by the car company (not surprisingly, Buick is the "official car" of the PGA Tour).

Faxon, who the week before had bummed a ride to the Memorial Tournament in Ohio on Greg Norman's plane, was practicing by himself on the green. Media attention was focused on such players as Paul Azinger, who had captured the Memorial with an improbable bunker shot. Surrounded by reporters after a practice round, Azinger made an observation that came across as a boast.

"It's so hard to win out here," he said. "I'm going to try to put last week behind me. I usually play poorly right after I win."

Elsewhere, too, the media put questions to Tom Kite, whose reign as U.S. Open champion had one more week to run. Often, such champions in the year following their victory play poorly. How had Kite dealt with this phenomenon? someone asked him.

Kite was stunned at what he considered the ignorance of the question. He had won two tournaments this season! "I've done a good job in handling it," he explained in a moment of self-absorption.

I felt like a failure. Having prepared myself beforehand with a constant diet of golf books, golf magazines, and golf viewing, there was not a single question I could think of at that moment to ask Kite that would break through the wall of self he had erected.

I would experience this feeling again during my sojourn on the tour. Other than during actual rounds, when initiating conversation with a competitor is expressly forbidden by PGA Tour media rules, it is very difficult to gauge when an interruption is appropriate—even, I found out, welcome. Most golfers do not want to talk after a tournament begins. Once, with the memory of my Westchester failure in mind, I waited an hour and a half for Tom Kite to complete a post-round practice session. Not a naturally talented athlete, Kite has achieved his success through repeated, dedicated practice, and I watched in some astonishment as he placed an iron on the ground, by his feet, to check his alignment and then later, on the practice green, putted until it was almost dark. Afterward I introduced myself, apologizing that it was the evening before the last round of a tournament, and Kite said he'd be happy to talk sometime—at the next tournament in which he played.

"Perhaps I could call you," I said.

"I don't want you calling me when I'm at home," he answered politely but very firmly, as if he had fielded countless such requests in his long career, which no doubt he had. "That would be taking time away from my family."

At Westchester, Brad Faxon said he'd meet me in a few minutes by the steps to the players' locker room, just off another putting green. We sat together on the steps, with Faxon greeting other players as they passed in and out. I mentioned running into Willie Wood, the Oklahoma player who won the 1983 Q-School, and whose wife, Holly, later died of cancer, leaving Wood with two young children to raise. Even before she died, Wood had started playing badly. I'd seen Brad at a tournament in New England around that time and asked him about Willie. And Brad had answered discreetly, "He's having some personal problems." Now Wood was competing again, trying to regain his old form while his in-laws took care of his children back home, and I had introduced myself to him on the green. Certainly I wasn't going to allude to the tragedy in his life, but I thought mentioning the Q-School might be a good icebreaker. "We met in Jacksonville Beach," I said to Wood, who nodded blankly. "We were staying at the same hotel."

That was a mistake, Brad explained to me as we sat on the steps. You didn't talk to a player like that "out here." This was the PGA Tour, and guys were meeting people every week.

What about Azinger, I wondered. "I met him at Q-School, too, Brad. He was in your group."

"Oh, man." Faxon shook his head.

"Yeah. So what about Norman?"

"Greg? Hah! You'll never get near him."

A YEAR LATER, Brad was again standing by the putting green at Westchester Country Club on a beautiful late-spring day, laughing with Norman about the extra-large shirts that Brad's caddie, Cubby, wore. Was Greg going to that night's Stanley Cup hockey game?

"No way I'd go," said Greg. "How would you get out of there?" he added, with reference to the anticipated crowd at Madison Square Garden. "I heard tickets were selling for five hundred dollars."

Steve and Frank Carpiniello, who had been serving as volunteer marshals at the tournament for fourteen and sixteen years, respectively, kept an eye on the golfers crowded into the small range fashioned out of one of the golf holes from another Westchester course not being used in the tournament. Faxon and Norman, who had been putting because they were shortly to tee off (in different groups), had already hit balls on the range. Almost without exception, players before a round do their range warm-up before moving onto the putting green, where most of them also practice chips and bunker shots.

While many fans at golf tournaments move from group to group, or stay at one hole where they can see all the groups over the course of a day's play, I had concluded that the best opportunity for seeking answers to the mystery of what distinguished the pros' game from my own lay in the repeated observation of a few golfers. There are so many different situations—an infinite number, really—that confront a golfer over the course of a golfing life. Each of these moments requires not only a certain kind of physical skill but, invariably, a commitment—emotional, mental, even spiritual—that, again over time, and in combination with other moments, reveals who a golfer is.

So it did not matter particularly to me that neither Faxon nor Norman played really well this first day of the 1994 Westchester tournament. I thought of the U.S. Open the year before, when Faxon had played poorly and Norman had not even made the cut. I remembered how hot it was that week and the tremendous crowds that had caused traffic congestion of unimaginable proportions on the turnpike leading to the course site. I remembered with great satisfaction how I had decided impulsively to cut around the traffic congestion on my way to the tournament and, though I had no directions or map, continue to the next exit, where I literally followed my nose and was able to locate the course with only a few wrong turns. The press tent at the Open that week seemed even more crowded than the highway, and writers were complaining about the bad food and the shortage of working space, something that never happened at Westchester, where even the cold cuts at the writers' buffet had been freshly cooked on the premises.

After a fast start, with three birdies on the Westchester front nine, Faxon made the turn at minus three. But despite another birdie on the back nine, three bogeys coming in left him at the end of the day with a score of just minus one. Norman, too, had an uneven round, with a second shot on the par-five finishing hole that went into a hedge by the starter's tent at the adjacent first hole. Norman had to take an unplayable lie, at a penalty of one stroke, and drop his ball with the hedge blocking his view of the green. He made a beautiful pitch, to great cheers, and sank the putt for an incredible par.

I saw the Shark the next day during his post-round practice session on the putting green, where he repeatedly made two-foot putts before stopping to chat with Fred Couples. Couples, whose bad back had prevented him from defending his victory that spring in the Honda Classic, had only recently returned to the tour. While Greg and Freddie chatted, Greg's caddie, Tony Navarro, picked up Greg's Ping putter and sank several putts of his own. Then the Shark returned, working on putts in the six-to-eight-foot range, which he followed with several at a length of twenty feet. He made three in a row before trying a few downhill ten-footers. Another pro, John Huston, came by and took a few swings with a wedge. Each time the ball backed up three or four feet after hitting the green. Norman seemed oblivious to what was happening next to him, as did Tony, whose off-white shirt had shark-teeth patterns on its collar. Neither paid attention to anyone else on the green.

"Well, I'm going to work out," said Greg to Tony. "Then I'll pick up my family." Putting on a pair of eyeglasses with green lenses, Norman then strolled off the green past several startled fans and walked to the fitness trailer that was parked on the other side of the clubhouse entrance. A few other players remained near the green, one of them doing an imitation of Tom Watson's pathetic putting stroke, which, again, had cost him in that day's play.

Most golfers are superstitious, and all of them, when something is not going well, will look for a reason or person to blame their golf problems on. A golf writer's worst nightmare is to be accused by a player at a tournament of contributing to a bad shot. I wanted to watch golf as intimately as possible, and I had been able at many tournaments to secure a photographer's armband, which permitted me to follow golfers in competition while walking within the ropes that line the fairways and surround the greens and tees to keep the public at least an arm's length from their heroes.

In the past year, I had walked many rounds within the ropes while Greg Norman played. Completely focused on his game, he had never acknowledged me during a round. This enabled me to move almost invisibly, or so I thought, as he made his way from tee to green, green to next tee, green to range, and range to tee. Once when I said hello to him afterward he had looked up and replied, "How you doing, fellas." I turned around to check; there was no one behind me.

Because I knew Brad Faxon, I had been forced to adopt a different strategy in my golf-watching with him. While I felt that any player who was good enough to be playing professionally could perform with all sorts of distractions taking place around him, I also understood that any possibility of watching Faxon play golf for a period of time would end if, say, I were ever to find myself in his sight line as he was about to address a ball on the tee. Therefore, while I followed him on the course, I usually stood behind a few other people or even a tree. Except during pro-ams, when he sometimes invited me to walk with him, I never followed him inside the ropes.

More than once these precautions struck me as folly. And what was it that I was trying to find? Because someone played golf superbly, did that bequeath on the moments of golf action something transcendent? If the Shark had won the Tour Championship, would I be any closer to an understanding of the same?

Portland, Oregon

I'VE COME OUT here for the Fred Meyer Challenge, an unofficial invitational team tournament that Peter Jacobsen runs in his hometown. It's a two-day affair played at a course that Jacobsen helped design. The invitees play in pairs, and this year one of the guests is John Daly, who in his reply to most questions manages to use the verb "sucks."

Long before Daly arrived in Portland he had already earned a dubious reputation as the Roseanne of the golf tour. You never knew what he was going to say or do next, but chances were good that it would be something shocking, at least by the staid standards of professional golfers. So when Daly turned to face the crowd that filled the natural amphitheater around the eighteenth green of the Oregon Golf Club, during a pre-tournament exhibition, no one seemed surprised as he teed up a ball, his driver in hand, his apparent intent to hit his ball over the crowd. But certainly that was as far as even John Daly would go. Certainly even a man of Daly's poor judgment would not actually attempt to drive a golf ball over a crowd of several thousand people, when the slightest mistake in his swing could produce a shot that could easily kill someone.

Never a man to waste time, Daly took his stance, brought his club back way past parallel, and before Jacobsen or anyone else had a chance to stop him, swung from his heels and sent his ball high over the crowd, over the concession tents behind the crowd, all the way to a parking lot several hundred yards away. There was a hushed silence, then loud, prolonged yelling, whether out of relief or in excitement it was hard to tell. Daly smiled, while Jacobsen stared at him in fury.

Eventually, Daly would leave the tour on an enforced sabbatical, after several other incidents that seemed prompted by the same apparent disregard for other people. This was ironic, because Daly is also known as a soft touch. When he won the 1991 PGA Championship as the last alternate to get into the tournament, he donated a portion of his check to the family of a man fatally struck by lightning during the tournament.

Among the stars that were playing at the 1993 U.S. Open, John Daly received the most attention because he was able to get to the seventeenth green, a 630-yard par five, in two strokes. No one else, not even Greg Norman (who missed the cut), did that.

IT'S LATE SUMMER in Portland and the weather is overcast and on the chilly side. The course sits on a bluff overlooking the Willamette River. The wind from the river coming up and across the water, which runs in a deep gorge, makes goose bumps on my arms as I walk along the fairways watching Tom Weiskopf, a former star who now plays on the Senior Tour, and Chi Chi Rodriguez, his partner in this event, and Ben Crenshaw, 1984 Masters champion (sneaking a cigarette now and then), and Brad Faxon, whose drive on the first hole, uphill, is excellent, right in the middle of the fairway, which he follows with a fine approach—the first is a par five—and then a wedge which he hits past the flagstick, blowing stiffly in the breeze, before two-putting for a par. There is an extraordinary feeling of immense space here, accentuated by the spectacular view of snow-capped Mount Hood in the distance. What a contrast between that view and the signs promoting Marlboro cigarettes, which are the sponsors of a skins game the pros are playing in addition to the tournament competition. A nice stand of oaks and firs lines the fourteenth. I can see what must be a great salmon hole deep in the gorge below the ninth. How steep it is down that bank! How dark the water! Before this land became a golf course it was a farm. Before it was a farm it was forest.

In the press tent, where he has already finished his round, Fuzzy Zoeller watches host Peter Jacobsen chip on a television monitor showing the golfers still in competition. The look on Zoeller's face is one of total disinterest. Freddie Couples comes into the tent, takes a seat in the audience, and listens while Davis Love answers a few more questions from the stage. Freddy picks up a newspaper and reads it for thirty seconds or so; then he takes the stage, where he uses such words as "aggressive" in his answers to questions about how he believes this course needs to be played. Ben Crenshaw follows Couples to the stage.

"I'm playing terrible," says Crenshaw, sipping on a cup of coffee.

A sign outside the tent says, "No autographs inside media compound."

Media compound? This little tent we're sitting in?

Despite the media compound rules, someone asks Arnold Palmer for an autograph. He seems annoyed, but he obliges. The king of golf wants to get back to the putting green. Tom

Kite and Davis Love hit balls on the range, with its panoramic vista of the river valley and Mount Hood. Davis comes over to Kite to watch Kite swing and to give him a tip about his swing mechanics. They work together on Kite's takeaway. A couple of hundred yards away, identical Camrys are parked in a long row for the players to use while they are here in Oregon for the tournament (Toyota is one of the tournament sponsors).

At night, at a banquet held for all the tournament patrons, many of whose companies have spent several thousand dollars for them to be here, there are no hors d'oeuvres served with drinks. The dinner is held in a huge tent supported by aluminum struts. The floor of the tent has been assembled long enough for grass to have already grown in between the cracks. Colored cellophane streamers have been hung in a sad attempt to decorate the tent. The place is slow to fill up; by seven, when the dinner is supposed to begin, there are still many empty seats, despite the fact that the dinner was billed as a sellout. Dress is casual, which in this crowd means for most men a business suit with a colorful tie or an open-necked wide-collared shirt, perhaps with a gold necklace showing at the throat. Some of the sponsors are identified by table signs, such as *General Foods—Cool Whip*. Tom Weiskopf, looking hearty and, without a jacket, refreshingly informal, says as he sips a beer that he hit some good shots today.

"But I didn't know how to play the course," he says. "It's the first time I played the course." In fact, Weiskopf is here as a substitute. He happened to be in Seattle for another golf function a week before he accepted Jacobsen's request when another of the participants withdrew.

Tall, with a smile that reveals a healthy set of teeth, Weiskopf still speaks with a little bit of the Midwestern soothingness of his Ohio childhood and student days at Ohio State University. Perennially known as the man who kept finishing second to Jack Nicklaus in many head-to-head encounters, particularly in major championships, Weiskopf once took a score of twelve on the par-three eleventh at Augusta. Today, he returns to Augusta as a telecaster for CBS Sports. He seems comfortable with his seniordom. He doesn't play in many senior events, in part because he has a thriving golf-course-design business. It's also clear he likes to spend time with his wife, Jeanne, an outgoing, engaging woman who followed him hole by hole during the first round of the Fred Meyer Challenge, in which Weiskopf and Rodriguez finished last.

The next day, with a chance to finish first with his partner Rick Fehr, Brad Faxon pulls his drive on the eighteenth hole into the creek that runs along its left side. After this bad shot, he slams his club into the ground. Fehr hits a bad drive too, pushing his shot to the right, and he, too, slams his club. Now, instead of the birdie one of them expected to make, they're fighting for a team bogey. In the last group, Tom Purtzer also pushes his drive, while his partner, Steve Elkington, hits the fairway, as does Jim Gallagher, Jr., playing with partner Bruce Lietzke (who pulls his drive). The action is recorded by a crew from ESPN, which is leaving immediately after the tournament for an event in Hawaii. By the time these last players reach the green, both teams have a chance to win, but it looks like the Gallagher/Lietzke duo is in better shape, because Gallagher has only a four-foot putt, while Elkington has one of at least fifteen feet. Elkington makes his, and Gallagher misses. Watching from the fringe, dressed in blue jeans, John Daly looks on impassively.

Greg Norman is not here. Partnered with Gary Player, Norman actually finished in a tie for first in this tournament, the first year it was held, 1986. He has returned four times since, winning a total of $151,000. Norman, too, hosts his own tournament, though it actually appears on the PGA Tour schedule as an official, post-season event called the Franklin Funds Shark Shootout. Held in November at the Sherwood Country Club north of Los Angeles, the tournament is also a team affair, in this case over a period of three days. Just as Norman has played in Jacobsen's tournament (partnered in 1995 with Brad Faxon, his team would win in sudden death), Jacobsen has been a frequent participant in Norman's.

AT THE EIGHTEENTH tee at the Oregon Golf Club the view gives a person the sense of being inside a huge hollow, almost a tunnel with the top torn off. The course, designed by Peter Jacobsen, is a private club the rest of the year; as is the case at so many PGA Tour courses such as the Olympic Club, the public can enter only during a tournament. In Portland, where there had not been a tour event for more than a generation, this unofficial tournament drew large crowds and attracted considerable attention in the local press. The national press didn't pay attention, but the players did, because they earn big bucks for these boondoggles. In Jacobsen's tournament all a player's expenses were covered and last place was still worth $45,000 per team. In some of the overseas tournaments, even regular events on other tours, appearance fees as high as $250,000 are sometimes paid to Greg Norman and a very few other top players for competing.

Part of the reason for the Portland success was the force of Jacobsen's personality, which could be felt not only in the way the tournament was organized—the auction at the tournament dinner, for example, was a Jacobsen idea—but also in the quality of the field. Jacobsen, himself, was something of an anomaly, having won only four tournaments (until 1995, when he would actually lead the money list for several months after capturing two early-season titles; Jacobsen would ascribe the turnaround in his game to the improvement in his short game, for which he would credit the work of his teacher, Dave Pelz).

As she followed her husband around the course during the tournament, Jeanne Weiskopf carried with her a book to read during slow moments. She said that Tom found Senior Tour play to be slow and the setup of many of the Senior Tour courses to be too easy. Though Tom had the reputation when he was a regular tour player of being on occasion ill-tempered, here at Jacobsen's tournament he was the model of the happy golfer, except when he got in trouble on the course. He tossed his golf club at his bag after missing an approach shot on the fourteenth hole. Overall, Weiskopf played extremely well, hitting his tee shots very long and making many very accurate iron shots into the greens, but like Paul Moran he two-putted too often.

Sherwood Oaks, California

IT'S THE WEEK before Thanksgiving 1993. Brad Faxon is hitting balls on the range at Sherwood Oaks. His wife, Bonnie, will be flying in tomorrow with their two daughters, and the whole family will then head to Australia for three weeks after this tournament, where Brad will be competing in several tournaments. This will be their last such trip during the school year as a family; the following year their older daughter will enter kindergarten. Homes "starting at $500,000 to $550,000" are promoted behind the gates here at the country club. Many of them narrowly missed being burned to the ground during recent terrible brush fires that engulfed much of the land along the majestic southern California coast.

Faxon is fooling with a wedge that Nick Price has lent him. He hits five balls in a row over a deep bunker, through two trees, and onto a semi-elevated green, where each of the balls stops with terrific backspin.

"Isn't it soft?" says Nick when Faxon returns the club to him.

"Hey, I've got no cash," says Peter Jacobsen to Arnold Palmer, as they discuss a bet for the match. Overhearing this exchange, an expansive Greg Norman smiles. He is relaxed today. This is his party, and only his friends are here. All the marshals in this tournament are wearing black Shark shirts, black Shark hats, and black Shark jackets.

"Hey, Davis," the Shark says to Davis Love. "Davis, did you sell your boat yet?"

Love nods his head.

"What did you get for it?"

Love cites a figure of several hundred thousand dollars. Norman thinks the amount sounds too low.

"Hey, that's almost what I paid for it," Love says. "And they let me keep all the tackle."

John Cook arrives, a replacement for Paul Azinger, who has dropped out because of a shoulder injury that will later be diagnosed as curable cancer. "Call me Zinger," Cook smiles. He got here, he says, by helicopter.

Out on the course, Arnold Palmer and Greg Norman don't play their second shots on number one, because Arnold's drive is short, Greg's in a bunker. On the second, Greg hits another great drive. He takes his golf glove off between his shots. Many of the players do this.

This has been another bittersweet season for the Shark, whose victory in the British Open in July was followed by near victory in the PGA Championship in August and the crippling loss to Jim Gallagher, Jr., at the Tour Championship. Many people declared the Shark's last round at the British Open was the greatest round of his life. Some people went so far as to call it the greatest round ever played in a major championship by anyone, but this kind of hyperbole is common in golf as well as other sports. Just yesterday, Norman won the PGA Grand Slam of Golf, in which the winners of golf's four major championships get to compete against one another. Usually a two-day tournament, it was contested in one day, with morning and afternoon rounds, in order to accommodate Norman's need to be present for the Shark Shootout.

Not on the official Shark Shootout schedule, a chipping contest develops on the range between Brad Faxon and the young phenom Tiger Woods. Woods at this time has not yet won the 1994 and 1995 United States Amateur titles, but he has already competed as a high school student in some PGA Tour events, and he knows many of the players, including Faxon. Woods isn't playing in the Shark Shootout; he's just come by to watch the players, most of whom he knows. And they all know him, the most touted amateur since Jack Nicklaus.

"Hey, Greg, can I borrow this?" Faxon asks Norman. He wants to borrow the Shark's sand wedge for Woods.

"Yeah, sure," says the Shark.

Faxon and Woods walk to an area adjacent to the range, where a practice green with several flagsticks is guarded by a number of bunkers. Faxon gathers some golf balls by his feet and issues a challenge.

"All right, we'll go closest to the first pin, and you can't land the ball until it reaches the green."

Holding Norman's wedge, which is unusually heavy, Tiger smiles and nods.

"Oh," adds Faxon. "You get two points for a sink." He means you get double if you hole your shot.

After five shots each, Woods leads Faxon by a score of 3–2. With each shot, the player who won the previous one calls the next, as in "Now you have to hit the ball to the back pin, but you have to land it in the left rough." This is a fairly ridiculous sequence, but in spirit with the occasion.

Soon the score is 5–4, Woods still ahead.

"Okay, front pin, got to land it short," says Tiger. The score is tied before Woods pulls ahead again, 7–5. Eventually he wins, 11–9, but the end of the contest seems anticlimactic because Faxon, who has to leave, seems to hurry.

IN THE 1988 U.S. Open, held in Boston in June heat at a course so old and stodgy it is called The Country Club, Curtis Strange needed to get up and down from a deep bunker at the eighteenth to force a playoff with Nick Faldo. He made the shot and he made the putt, and the next day he beat Faldo in the eighteen-hole playoff. The following year in Rochester, when Tom Kite faltered, Strange won his second consecutive U.S. Open title.

Now, in Thousand Oaks, California, in late November, on

the practice range of Sherwood Oaks Country Club, Strange hit balls, looking for the swing that had brought him those two major titles. (He would still be looking gallantly for that swing at the 1995 Ryder Cup, when he needed a par on any of the last three holes to clinch a U.S. victory.) He hadn't won on tour since the 1989 Open. After each swing he watches the ball disappear into the twilight. Then he hits another. Then he watches. Sometimes he takes a break to talk with the person next to him. Tiger Woods's father is watching Strange, and Strange greets him.

"How you doing, Mr. Woods," Strange says with the courtliness of his Virginia upbringing. And the two men speak for a few minutes about Tiger's decision to attend Stanford. Then Strange continues hitting balls. He is working on his long irons.

Setup. Swing. Watch.

Setup. Swing. Watch.

AS THE SUN falls behind the Coast Ranges the temperature quickly becomes chilly, and everyone seems in a hurry to get to dinner, a players-only affair at the house where Norman is staying.

Two nights before there was a banquet in the clubhouse, primarily for the patrons and sponsors whose money defrayed the tournament's cost. Like the tournament itself, the banquet was organized by International Management Group, which at the time still represented Norman. I had been invited to attend the tournament by an IMG representative whom I had met several months before in Florida, but now, with the pressure of performing while his client was present, this man had forgotten.

"Sorry," said a message waiting for me that day in my hotel room. "Won't be able to accommodate you for dinner tonight."

Later, in the lobby of the Hyatt in Thousand Oaks, several of the golfers gather with some television announcers before going out for dinner. Natty Jim Nance from CBS and Nick

Price in the kind of jacket that a person would wear if he were fishing walk through the lobby, followed by Gary McCord. The familiarity of players and announcers is not forced. They see one another on the road all year, and they need one another to succeed. There would be no tour as we know it without television coverage.

Price, whose low-key demeanor and quiet cheerfulness might mark him as a guidance counselor at school, is leaving for South Africa after the tournament. He will remain there through the coming holidays, except, probably, to play in the Johnnie Walker in Jamaica just before Christmas. Norman has already pulled out of that event, saying he needs the time with his family. In fact, he is about to break formally with his agent, IMG, which organized the Jamaica tournament.

An entire year of amusing negotiation by phone and fax will pass before I am cleared for a private, personal Shark interview. By then Norman would be getting ready to announce his ill-fated World Tour, having already set up his own management company, Great White Shark Enterprises, with an old Australian friend, Frank Williams, in charge. Williams, who likes to praise what he calls his employer's attention to detail, reflects on the "difficulty of *being* Greg Norman." He says, "I wouldn't want to do it for a day."

"IF THE SPORT ever closed down, professionally, I would always play golf with my friends," Norman confessed to me one day. "I would always go out for a Sunday or a Saturday or a Wednesday afternoon with my buddies. When I'm in Australia, I do it all the time. Over here I don't, because I don't know that many people over here."

As a boy growing up in Queensland, Australia, the son of a mining engineer named Mervyn, Greg Norman started playing golf through the influence of his mother, Toini. A four-handicapper, she played when she was pregnant with Greg. As a teenager, he caddied for her, and, according to Shark legend, he finally tried hitting the ball himself when he was sixteen. In two years he was a scratch golfer, as a result of his natural athletic coordination and strength, a fierce desire to excel that manifested itself in long hours practicing, and the opportunity to learn from the teaching pro at Royal Queensland Golf Club in Brisbane, Charlie Earp. Norman's first golf job after high school graduation was as Earp's assistant. His rise through the ranks was rapid. At the age of twenty-one, only five years after taking up the game, he won his first tournament in Australia as a professional. Eventually he gravitated to the Asian and European tours, where he was also successful, before finally coming to the United States, where he first played full-time in 1984. He won the Kemper Open that year and very nearly won the U.S. Open. Two years later, when he had the distinction of being the leader at the start of the final round of all four major championships (he was still the leader at the end in just one, the British Open), the Shark had been crowned the best golfer in the world. He was thirty-one.

MY OWN GOLFING career began when I realized my father was dying. My father was never a golfer, but he was a great one for giving advice, and many of his favorite words and expressions could be applied with good effect to the game. The most important thing in life, he used to tell me, is tempo, a concept that was at the root of his perceptions about people and what they do and how they get along. When I was practicing the piano as a boy, he always told me to get the rhythm right.

In golf, people will often refer to a rhythmic swing, but when they discuss the pace of a player's overall play the word "tempo" is employed. I remember happening on the great LPGA player Beth Daniel, who was practicing on the range one Saturday afternoon at a tournament in Vermont. She was hitting at the far end of the range, which was actually a teaching facility for the golf course where the tournament was being held. Most of the other golfers had finished for the day; a few were still on the course or the smaller range adjacent to it.

The range area where Beth Daniel was hitting looked as if it had been fashioned from a hay mowing. She was hitting, really, in a very large field or meadow. Woods bordered the cleared land, and a pond lay to her left. It was late summer and, in the mountains, the air at this hour was cool.

Beth Daniel hit ball after ball with a graceful, powerful, very athletic swing. She had great tempo, too. She watched the flight path of each shot before selecting another ball from the pile near her feet for the next shot. A friend—perhaps her caddy—sat nearby, on the ground, but they spoke very little. I watched Daniel hitting balls for twenty minutes before it was clear she was finished and an interruption might be inoffensive. I introduced myself and praised the rhythm of the routine I had just witnessed.

"You must be playing well," I volunteered. "Where do you stand after today's round?"

"Actually, I didn't make the cut," Daniel replied. "I'm just here because it's easier to leave when I was originally planning to, after the tournament ends.

"Golf is a funny game," she continued. "In any other sport, once you've got it, it stays. But in golf, how you do comes and goes." And she shook her head.

I thought afterward of something Greg Norman said in Florida, a year before he shot a record twenty-four under par to win the Players Championship. Complimenting him on a good round, a reporter had asked him to explain his success that day, and the Shark had credited the light.

The light? It had been slightly overcast, with no direct sun.

"Yeah. This was a good light to play golf. Depth perception was good."

Trying to analyze his own achievement at the same tournament, on a course famous for its number and kind of hazards, Nick Price was virtually silent.

"When you're playing well you don't see the trouble," he finally offered.

"Okay, Nicky," the Shark said to him another time. This was

in Augusta, after a practice round for the Masters, and Greg had been hitting five-irons off the range by the practice green. A second, larger range there has no green, and he had been hitting the ball so well he began using that separate range, located on the other side of the club's tree-lined Magnolia Drive, as his target. His shots had to clear the trees or they might have struck the windshield of a green-jacketed member's car as it was driving up Magnolia Lane.

"Okay, Nicky," said the Shark when he spied his friend working on his short game. And Greg put a bill on the green, next to one of the practice holes.

"Let's see you hole that, Nicky," Greg said, and Nicky nearly did.

Three days later, after a Masters round when the light must have been wrong, Norman came off the eighteenth, where his ball had found a bunker, and walked straight to an informal press conference held impromptu on the spacious lawn that overlooked the green. He did not seem to see his wife, who had been standing near the green before he finished playing. He was in a hurry to get the questions over with and leave.

"The harder the golf course, the better it is for me," he said. And what about his round today? I asked him a few minutes later in the rarefied quiet of the Augusta clubhouse, where he went briefly to change out of his golf shoes.

"Shit happens."

WHEN I WAS a high school senior, my father wrote me a letter that closed with the instruction to look at myself in the mirror. That is exactly what a golf teaching pro told me to do a few years ago when I was having trouble getting rid of a slice.

I'm rarely able to concentrate completely over a full eighteen, which is a main reason for my so-so scores, but some of the things I daydream about while playing golf I see with great clarity. I can be standing on the tee of a par three, reminding myself to shift my weight to the inside of my right foot as I take the club back and to keep my head down as I come back through, and suddenly I'll remember my father's campaign when I was a teenager for me to gain some weight. I was a skinny kid and, after eighth grade, had stopped growing, and he didn't think this was healthy. So for about a month one spring he gave me money to buy a milkshake each day at a restaurant around the corner from our house. I didn't add a pound.

Like the good golfer who doesn't boast of his scores or the poor one who realizes no one is interested in his troubles, my father accepted his public successes with modesty. And, so far as I can make out, he never spoke openly with anyone about a personal problem or worry. He might sometimes tell me a story that was partially revealing of an incident in his or someone else's life, but the preface or final line was always "Keep this one to yourself."

It was the very opposite kind of remark you hear among golfers at a tournament, where knowledge is passed around so liberally. There are no secrets. You could tell a person everything Greg Norman has paid Butch Harmon to tell him and that person would still be an unlikely candidate to win next week's tournament.

"I LIVED BY the putter earlier in my career, I died by it today," Tom Watson said mournfully, after losing the 1994 AT&T National Pro-Am at Pebble Beach to fellow veteran—and now television announcer—Johnny Miller. This was the same Pebble Beach tournament in which comedian Bill Murray's antics as Scott Simpson's amateur partner upset both the humorless Watson and then PGA Tour commissioner Deane Beman.

"Who's got a big mouth?" I overheard Murray ask a fan in the gallery on Saturday.

"I do," a woman with blond hair spoke up.

Murray, who was wearing a sport jacket, gave the woman his golf ball and said, "Open it up and wash this off for me."

If Watson lost the tournament with his painfully bad putting on Sunday, Miller won it with his iron play early in the third round on Saturday. He was playing in one of the first groups, probably because his amateur partner was NBC announcer Bryant Gumbel and they would finish before the telecast came on the air on CBS.

My notes for that round, scribbled in the early-morning chill of a gray northern California day at a course that literally hangs over the Pacific in places, are hard to decipher.

"See J. Miller draw ball on three."

"Wedge to seven or eight feet."

"Another fine drive at four, a low fader."

"Stiff again at five. Another birdie, that's four in a row."

Without reference to those notes, or the abundant stories I saved from newspapers and golf magazines, I have little recollection of the golf action. I see, instead, the way Watson's shoulders slumped after he missed a putt on Sunday at the seventeenth, the same hole where, a few minutes before, Miller had closed the face of his four-iron, because he carried no three, and hit a magnificent shot into the wind.

And I see the figure of 1964 U.S. Open champion Ken Venturi, at the tournament to work the telecast, filming some sort of a promotion at the eighteenth tee after the Friday round. It was sunny that day, and the breeze coming off the ocean was invigorating, the view from the tee thrilling.

After his filming was complete, Venturi turned to face the water. He was holding either a driver or a three-wood in one hand, a few golf balls in the other. He teed up one of the balls, took a swing, and sent the ball over the waves, toward an outcropping of rocks that formed a very small island about four hundred yards offshore.

The ball landed in the ocean. Venturi teed up another.

"Hit the island," said a security guard.

"If I could, I'd be playing in this tournament."

MY FATHER AND I spoke on the telephone just a few days before he died, and he said he wanted to visit us. We settled on a date, and then we discussed what we might do when he came. He had a bad leg from a car accident, but he stressed that this wouldn't prevent his participation in whatever we planned.

"We can rent a cart," he said. "That way I can go out with you when you play golf."

Those were my father's last words to me.

The first round I played after his death, golf seemed a very trivial activity. I played the round in a kind of trance, swinging mechanically and not caring about my score. I'd never played better, and the experience taught me something new about the game, I thought.

Recently, I played golf with a friend whose handicap is in the low single digits, and on the front nine I had three mini-disasters that, I concluded, would cost me the chance of having a good round. After the turn, I bogeyed the tenth and eleventh, and my third shot on the twelfth—a long par four—was over the green.

My lie was on a small hill, in deep grass, and I took my sand wedge to see if I could extricate myself from the mess I was in. I swung and the ball started off to the right, then landed on the fringe and began rolling to the left, toward the pin, until it disappeared into the hole.

"Touch" is a word you hear often in golf conversation. My father, who never did anything athletic—for fear, he said, that he would hurt his hand and not be able to play the organ—would have understood what was meant by touch, for the quality of being gentle came to him naturally. The best players all have touch, and even many average golfers score well because they have good touch around the greens. I've played with older men who hit the ball off the tee fifty yards shorter than I do, and yet they can beat me because, inside one hundred yards, they consistently get the ball so close to the pin. The secret of touch in golf is to strike the ball gently but with authority, not overswinging, yet not freezing halfway through the swing.

I played the last six holes in three over par and was so elated that I went out the next morning with my son to repeat my success. I got into trouble early and never recovered, and my score after nine holes was my poorest of the season.

"Don't worry about your damn score," former Massachusetts state amateur champion Tracy Mehr tries to convince his pupils. Mehr, a college coach in several sports, remained competitive until an accident with a lawn mower badly injured one of his eyes. But he continues to play golf almost every day, dispensing tips and good humor and searching for his youthful distance off the tee, now elusive.

"What do you mean?" I asked him. I had just taken a triple bogey and felt my day's round was ruined. I was fearful of continuing. "Don't you keep score when you play?" I asked.

"Not until I'm done," he replied.

"How do you remember it?" I asked.

"That's easy. I can tell you each shot you've taken today. You don't forget."

"What do you think about, then?" I persisted.

"For one thing, that I'm damn lucky to be out here. And so are you."

"Yes?"

"And I think about the flight of the ball, the way it takes off from the tee. I like to watch it. I like to see what it does in the wind, feel the wind in my face."

One of the reasons I play golf, I suppose, is that it is so unlike my father. Yet, playing sometimes more than I should, I realize that I haven't escaped his influence. Too much of a good thing. When I think about my father and what he did with his life, I believe that in his great enthusiasm for music, his friends, and family, he never knew when to say "Enough," when to guard his desire to give too much to the moment before it was overwhelmed with an emotion it could not sustain. This, too, is true in the pursuit of the little white ball; success can breed not success, but failure, as the golfer, charged with the euphoria of a well-hit three-iron or a perfectly stroked putt, chases the next shot with an excitement that negates the achievement preceding it.

As the Shark would say, as soon as you think you've got it, it's gone.

THERE THE SHARK is now, coming up the fourth at Cromwell, where they play the Greater Hartford Open. He's even for the day. He's playing here because to receive permission from the commissioner's office to play the year before, 1993, in a tournament in Japan that conflicted with a PGA Tour event he promised to come to Connecticut. He looks bored and tired, not at all as he did the third round of the Tour Championship, the day before the late collapse that gave the tournament to Jim Gallagher, Jr. That day he played the fateful sixteenth conservatively and scored a par, which he followed with a birdie at the seventeenth, a birdie that was set up by a good drive and then a three-wood that ran up the throat of the green, the ball coming to rest about ten feet from the pin, in the back center. He very nearly made his first putt for eagle. Then on eighteen, the hole where he would overclub himself the next day, he hit a fine drive and followed it with a fabulous wedge 108 yards, which landed two feet from the hole.

"Exaggeration," Peter Jacobsen would say later. "That is the key to improvement."

"Exaggeration and repetition," Judy Rankin corrected him.

Neither explained how Greg Norman might have altered his San Francisco fate, or redirected that year's two painful putts at the PGA, both on the eighteenth hole (one in regulation, one in a playoff), both of which almost went in, or replayed the final round of the 1993 Masters, birdieless after the second hole.

Earlier in his career, the Shark under pressure occasionally came out of his swing and blocked a shot right. Curing this tendency had been one of the principal reasons for his seeking the help of Butch Harmon. But the mental obstacle was the biggest to overcome. This is invariably the case with a golfer at the professional level—how to find a way to do in competition what he can already do in practice. While practicing, he is always asking, Is my swing good enough to hold up in a close tournament?

BACK HOME FOR a few days in Rhode Island, where he had moved with his family from Florida, Brad Faxon stopped by his favorite tailor's to have some jeans altered, then looked up his old teacher, Joe Benevento, at the private East Providence country club, Metacomet, where Benevento was the pro (and where Brad's father was a member). The day before, Faxon had been "striping the ball," but he wanted to make some adjustments to a driver he was thinking of using. He needed Benevento's help to install several different kinds of shafts on a number of driver heads, so he could try them all out.

"Would a two-point-two torque be any heavier than a one-point-nine?" he asked.

"I've got a book," replied Benevento. "I think it's lighter."

About to turn fifty, Benevento had the complexion of a man who had lived his life outdoors. He spoke with a quiet voice, in contrast with the assertive, sometimes insistent tone of Faxon. His eyes were deeply set and the hollows around them reflective of the dream he had been chasing since Brad Faxon was an infant. He wore a golf jacket, zippered, with the collar turned up in the autumn air. Benevento had played a few tour events in the 1970s but had never been good enough to be a successful professional player. He was trying to decide if he should attempt to qualify for the Senior Tour. He was concerned about spending the money to register for the qualifying events.

"Hey, Joe," Faxon said. "You don't use a five-minute epoxy?"

The two men were talking in Benevento's repair shop, located off a practice green. Cubby, who was staying with Brad en route to Fred Couple's caddy's wedding in Connecticut, was out on the course, playing a few holes.

"I like to come here and play, too," Faxon said. "I like to play places I am familiar with. Then, on tour, when I'm playing holes that I'm not comfortable with, I try to visualize something here. Say a cut shot on four."

Benevento set the clubs aside so the glue could dry overnight. He'd been having trouble with his putting, and he wondered if Brad would look at his stroke. The men walked outside. Benevento's wife, Maryann, followed. The deadline for applying for Senior Tour qualification was tomorrow, and the fee was a hefty $2,000.

"How've you been driving them?" Faxon asked Benevento.

"I'm longer," Benevento said. "Aren't I, Maryann?"

As I watched Brad Faxon correct his golf teacher's putting stance, I remembered walking back to the second hole at Augusta the year before to study the path of Norman's birdie chip. Wondering if it might have continued off the green had it not gone in the hole, I walked up the hill of the second fairway, reversing the direction the golfers took, and did not turn around until I had reached a small brook hidden in the woods, which were filled, then, with flowers and blossoming shrubs.

Perhaps, in his analysis of the year, Norman had replayed this round, too. Perhaps he, too, is stalking the Shark. Whenever he plays golf professionally, he always has to think about the damn score, as Tracy Mehr would say. He has to think about the collapse at Olympic and the near-wins in the majors and the carping of his critics, including many of the men against whom he competes. And each time he tees it up he has to compete with an image of himself for which he is ultimately responsible.

"Andre Agassi is to me the best at that," he told me. "I don't know him, never met him, but he portrays the image that he's built of himself so well that it's going to stay with him always.

He'll always be himself. He's a genius at that. I'm sure that off the tennis court he's a totally different type of guy."

While Andre Agassi no longer has a burden of the past to carry with him onto the court, Greg Norman's entire career still seemed cast in retrospective promise. But you can't play golf backwards. In golf, as my father taught me in life, memory is a late imagination.

SHARKBITE

SOMETIMES ALL THE parts of your game don't gel all at one time. One year the best part of my game might have been my short game. You've always got someting to work on, no question about it. Whether it's a short game or long game or whatever. It's something you work on over Christmas or the holiday break. Because you know if you don't come out ready to play the following year, then these guys are going to fly on by you, and if you start the year off on a bit of a backward note, where you haven't prepared yourself properly over the break, then you're really going to pay the price.

ANOTHER SECRET TO success is the people you have around you. All the great leaders of the world may be great in their own right, but they've surrounded themselves with great people. People they can trust. A CEO can be a great person but have a horrible board of directors who make some wrong decisions and the company will fail. If you have a wonderful board of directors making right decisions, the company will succeed. If the board of directors doesn't have the welfare of the company at heart, the company hurts, but if they have the welfare of the company at heart, it makes the CEO look great. So it's a matter of the CEO having the expertise to pick the right people to surround him.

I'm not saying that I'm an expert at picking the right people, but I've been fortunate in that I have great people around me. Some of my people I met through others, some I knew in Australia and just asked them to join me. I have good friends in the sport. There are some great people out there.

IF PEOPLE SAY they always want to play well when they play with me, that's a great compliment. Jack Nicklaus said to me one time when those guys were chipping in shots on me—I was over at his house, and he said, "Greg, don't forget, I've been through all that too. You've always got to remember that the greatest compliment paid to you when you walk out on the first tee is people are going to elevate their games just to beat you."

Jack and I are good friends, absolutely. No one knows what happens behind the doors or outside the golf course. That's the disappointing thing about how some journalists portray us. Nobody else knows how you think or understand. When you go home and sit down with your friends, no one understands that. I'm not going to tell anybody because that's my private world.

People fabricate a lot of stuff that just isn't true. I'm alleged to have been on drugs, have cancer, and none of it has an ounce of truth in it. Relationships are lied about and are so far from the truth it's ridiculous. They talk about bad blood between me and Pete Dye, and it makes me very angry. Unfortunately, people receive a perception from what they read in a magazine or in the paper, and no matter what retraction is written you can't change that perception. And even when you call the reporter and ask him where he got his information and convince him it's so far from the truth, he writes a retraction, but it's too late. It doesn't matter. Your name has been tarnished.

That's a sad thing about being in the limelight. People are looking for a reason to drag you down. There's lots of jealousy in this world, unfortunately. But if you want success, you have to deal with all that stuff.

ATTACK
LIFE

THE STIR STARTED long before he had reached the Greater Hartford Open's tenth tee, his first that day. (During the first two days of most PGA Tour events, players begin their rounds on both the first and tenth tees, with those who tee off on the first on Thursday teeing off on the tenth on Friday, and vice versa, in order for everyone to have time to play before darkness.) On the GHO tee an official had just introduced Mark Calcavecchia, the 1989 British Open champion, playing in a threesome in front of the Shark. But Calcavecchia, instead of hitting his drive, looked up across the tee, past the scorer's tent, to the road that led from the clubhouse to the tee. There was a fence there, but he could not see it. Backed up three and four deep on both sides of the fence, people pressed against it and stood by the entrance to the tee and alongside the rope that stretched the length of the fairway. The crowd was too loud for Calcavecchia to be able to concentrate on his drive, so he waited for the shouts to subside. But it was not Calcavecchia for whom people were cheering (though he was one of the more popular players on tour).

The time was just after lunch on a hot, muggy June afternoon, less than a week since the Shark had lost the 1995 United States Open by two very painful strokes to Corey Pavin. No one had expected him to be competing at the GHO in Cromwell, Connecticut, just south of Hartford, so soon after the sadness of Shinnecock. But this was the best way to put the past behind him.

Play.

Focus.

Forget your troubles and move on.

He was a titan of trouble. Other athletes got into trouble at home, with drugs or alcohol, in cahoots with a gambler or even a thief. The sufferings of Greg Norman, which were common knowledge, came on the course: the four majors he had lost in playoffs, the tournaments that had been snatched away at the last moment. With his latest defeat at the Open he had now finished second in a major seven times.

Trouble indeed.

But Greg Norman was not one to dwell on negatives. More than any other golfer of his generation, he had put himself in a position to win each time he competed. In the 214 PGA Tour events he had entered in his career prior to Hartford, he had made the cut an astounding 197 times. (Three times in that career he had withdrawn before the completion of a tournament because of an injury.) In an amazing one out of every two tournaments he had entered since the start of his PGA Tour career, he had finished in the top ten.

The noise at the tenth tee grew louder. Still holding his driver, Mark Calcavecchia shook his head and smiled, then took his stance as Greg Norman burst through the crowd finally and, with a reflexive flapping of his arms, signaled to the throng around him to quiet down. But the noise began building again after Calcavecchia and his group had finished driving and it was time for Norman to be introduced.

From a slight distance he was looking as good as ever today; you had to be close to notice how drained he still seemed from the Open loss. Up close, Greg also looked smaller than you would think from watching him on television. His waist was extremely thin, and his shoulders extraordinarily broad. He spoke engagingly in his Australian drawl, rarely forgetting to smile for the ubiquitous cameras. But the lines on his face were more deeply etched, the hollows around his eyes more profoundly recessed. He works hard to stay in good shape; here in Cromwell, at the TPC at River Highlands, he had arrived with enough time to go through a long stretching and exercise routine before he hit a single golf ball. When he is not playing golf in a tournament, he works out at home under the supervision of a personal trainer. He is fanatical about taking care of himself physically, as though trying to hold off the effects of middle age, fast approaching (he had just turned forty). A little of the golden hair, so prominently sticking out over the ears and down the neck from under the black Shark hat he wore today, was receding, enough to give you a sense that he might eventually lose much of the hair on top of his head.

The image of a bald Shark was, of course, at odds with the glamorous figure Greg cut at the TPC at River Highlands as he prepared to hit his first drive.

At the tee, standing still or nervously twitching, golfers reveal something of their personalities. If you watch carefully, you can even detect something in the way a golfer sticks his tee into the ground.

Norman inspected the ball Tony Navaro had just given him.

GOLFERS WHO LOSE their composure during the heat of competition or otherwise do not perform up to their capabilities are called head cases. But everyone who plays professional golf is a head case. The successful pros are simply those who have learned to cope with a higher level of anxiety than their competitors. Inevitably, however, even the coolest customer on the tour cracks.

Playing in the 1995 Buick Invitational at San Diego, Brad Faxon and Phil Mickelson had each mistakenly played the other's golf ball during the second round. Their caddies had misidentified their drives, and neither player had checked before he hit his second shot. At the time, Brad was one stroke behind the tournament leaders. His mistake—hitting Mickelson's ball—cost him a two-stroke penalty, and he fell out of contention. After the round, he told Cubby that if anything like this ever happened again he would have to fire Cubby.

A few months later, in the first round of another tournament sponsored by Buick—the Buick Classic at Westchester—Faxon came to the last hole, a par five, at three under. Hoping to earn points that would place him on the United States Ryder Cup team, Brad wanted especially to have a good tournament at Westchester. A win at Westchester would virtually guarantee him a spot on the team that would go head to head against Europe's best the following fall.

Standing on the tee with his driver in one hand, he reached with his other for a ball from Cubby. His focus was on the fairway in front of him, a fairway that had a memorial plaque marking the spot from where Bob Gilder had once hit a three-wood into the hole for a double eagle and a tournament victory. Brad wasn't expecting a double eagle, but he did want to hit a good drive and follow it with a shot into the green that left him with a chance for eagle or a certain birdie.

Earlier in the week, at home, Brad had been practicing his drives, still the weakest part of his game. He'd been using a new Titleist ball, the Professional, during that practice session. At Westchester, however, he had switched back to his regular ball, the Titleist tour balata. Before leaving home he had reminded Cubby to clean out the Titleist Professionals from his bag, because under the rules a golfer cannot use two different kinds of balls in a round. He can, however, replace a ball with another of the same kind after he has holed out, or even while he is playing a hole if his ball is damaged. After bogeying the seventeenth at Westchester, Brad wanted a new ball. Cubby reached into the bag for one and handed it to Brad as Brad stood on the eighteenth tee gazing down the fairway. On one side, the ball was clearly marked Titleist. Neither Cubby nor Brad noticed anything else on the ball until, a few minutes later, the two men reached the green, and Brad bent over to mark his ball. When he picked it up he could not believe what he saw. Clearly stamped on the ball was the word "Professional."

Faxon immediately called for an official and told him what had happened, but he already knew what the official would say. So did Cubby, whose emotions were in turmoil. He had just bought a new house in Sun Valley. In only a few weeks Brad was playing in the United States Open, and Cubby was also looking forward to the British Open at St. Andrews later in the summer. Now, suddenly, he feared that he would not be going.

"Two strokes," the official said to Brad. "I'm sorry."

Faxon placed his ball back on the green, removed the marker, and putted. By the time he had holed out, his score on the hole was nine. Horrified, he told Cubby he would meet him shortly in the clubhouse.

Disconsolate, Cubby carried Brad's bag back to the clubhouse area, sat down, and started crying. Everything he had worked for: was he going to lose it, just because, somehow, an errant ball had escaped his cleaning out of the bag after the practice session with the Professionals?

"I'm going to handle this one a lot better than I handled San Diego," Faxon said. He had fired caddies before. But Cubby had been with him a long time now. The two men were friends. Cubby always seemed to know what to say—or when not to say anything—during pressured tournament moments. And Brad himself had been partly responsible for the nine on the last hole; Brad, not Cubby, had taken seven strokes (not counting the penalty).

Cubby kept his job, but not without some scars. Carrying Brad's bag from the last green after the second round in Hartford a month later, someone asked him what had happened in Westchester, and he froze.

"Don't talk about it," he said sternly and kept walking.

NOW, IN HARTFORD, Greg Norman flexed his knees slightly and bent at the waist before precisely pushing his tee into the ground. His focus on this simple action was complete, because the height of the tee was important to the success of the subsequent shot. With out of bounds on the right, he wanted to draw the ball here from right to left, so he teed the ball a little higher than he did when facing a fairway that was more forgiving than this one.

He stood behind the ball on its tee, focusing on his target. Then he took his stance and addressed the ball. He checked his grip pressure; if it was too loose in his left hand, he would slide his left thumb up the shaft a half inch or so.

Shifting his weight to his right side, he took his driver back and then started his downswing with his hips, the hands and the club following. The ball exploded off the clubface with tremendous velocity and flew on a right-to-left trajectory to a spot in the fairway more than three hundred yards away.

"Save it for Sunday, Greg!" a heckler hollered from behind the tee, but the Shark appeared not to hear.

Though professional golfers are by and large a fairly friendly lot, particularly in comparison to their colleagues in such team sports as baseball and basketball, there is still a good deal of superstition when it comes to getting a player to talk about the secret of his game. Many are reluctant to say too much for fear that, as if they were bragging about a discovery, they might pay dearly for the sin of hubris. In contrast to basketball players, there is also a kind of unstated ethic among the players that the average golfer should not stand out in a way that will draw attention to himself. Even the stars who do, especially Norman, can draw criticism simply for the attention they receive (Norman is one of the few who seem to enjoy the spotlight). It is hard to understand why an average player would criticize Greg Norman for generating the kind of publicity that increases the tour's profile and clearly enlarges the interest of the public in the tour and, correspondingly, the size of the purses paid (put up typically by the individual tournament sponsors, usually in tandem with whatever television network they have contracted with for that week's telecast). But it is easy to imagine how difficult it must be for a fellow competitor to stick to his game when playing with Greg.

He was paired these first two days with Kenny Perry and Rocco Mediate, two middle-level pros whose careers were headed in opposite directions at the moment. From Kentucky, the personable Perry had been on a hot streak this year, and his stated goal was to put most of his winnings into the public course he was building in his hometown. Mediate had missed much of the previous season recovering from back surgery, and he was still not completely healed.

"WITH NO WIND and calm conditions, the morning scores were relatively low," Kenny Perry's caddy told a reporter after yesterday's first round. "However, wind began to blow at noon, and that will make the rest of the day difficult," he said.

"We had a nice pairing, playing with Norman and Mediate. Norman hit the ball great, but his putter let him down. Mediate continues to struggle with his back, but he is making progress.

"The fifteenth hole will play a big part of this year's tournament. The hole is only three hundred yards, but it leaves you with a lot of options. Most guys are trying to drive the green. It's elevated about six feet, so it's difficult to get on the top. There are bunkers and water down the left side and woods and bunkers down the right. Keep an eye on this hole as the week goes on.

"Friday we play at one oh four p.m. The conditions will be

difficult and the wind is sure to blow. It will be a day of survival."

Today, Friday, Perry and Mediate were unfazed by the fuss. Over the next few hours, if anything distracted them, it was not the fans following the Shark but the golf gods who seemed to be hovering over him. Had anyone ever seen him hit the ball better?

His first drive was followed by an approach that left Greg with eight or nine feet for birdie. He just missed the putt and scored a par.

On the eleventh hole—his second—a par three, downhill, his nine-iron tee shot landed three feet from the pin. He made the birdie putt to go one under for the day and four under for the tournament (he had shot a three-under 68 the day before).

A uniformed policeman and two security guards whose usual gigs were rock concerts accompanied him to the twelfth tee, where he hit another terrific tee shot and then almost put his second shot, a nine-iron, in the hole. Tap-in for birdie. Two under for the day, five under for the tournament.

On thirteen, the Shark pulled his drive, though it still landed in the fairway. After thinking about going for the green in two—this was a par five, with a pond fronting the green—he chose to lay up with a long iron, and he pushed the shot right, into a bunker, fifty yards from the hole. For the first time in the round, he was in trouble.

But not for long. Hitting his pitching wedge and firing, as he would all day, directly at the flag, he stopped his ball six feet from the pin and made the putt for his third birdie in a row.

The wild cheering from the growing crowd swelled further with a Shark birdie on fourteen (after a putt of about three feet). It was as if the Shark were in the process of transforming his image into a legend. Simultaneously, Greg was the underdog and the favorite.

His drive to the green of the fifteenth hole, his sixth, a short par four, added to the great impression he was making. He had

had to wait on the tee while Calcavecchia's group reached the green and each player marked his ball. But there had been no waiting in Greg's decision to use his driver, even though a poor shot could have landed in the lake to the left and rear of the green.

At that green, Greg marked his ball, sixty feet from the hole, and then said to his caddy, "Tony, Tony, watch the golf bag. They're going to hit up." He was referring to the group behind him, now on the tee. After their shots, all short, Greg putted. His ball stopped several feet shy of the cup, and he missed the next one. Instead of a possible eagle or certain birdie, he would have to settle for par.

The tee shot at sixteen was slightly pushed—one of very few mistakes Greg would make all day. The ball landed in some long grass between a bunker and water, and Greg was unable to get up and down to save par on the hole. But he narrowly missed a birdie on seventeen before pushing his tee shot on eighteen, a par four whose fairway formed the floor of a nat-ural amphitheater where thousands of people could see the golf, most of them sitting on the ground but some, on the top of one side, watching from corporate tents.

There, corporate high-rollers and their guests could hobnob in an area restricted to people with the proper passes. These funny-looking structures represented a further financial un-derpinning of most tournaments, even including the most pres-tigious and, ostensibly, least-tainted-by-money event of the year, the United States Open. That tournament, run not by the PGA Tour but by the United States Golf Association, one of the two ruling bodies of golf (the other being the Royal and An-cient Golf Club at St. Andrews, Scotland), was the site of more corporate tents than any other, helping to generate a seven-fig-ure Open profit for the not-for-profit USGA.

Greg Norman was not distracted by the sight of corporate tents. The way he had been playing, he was aware of almost nothing but his golf ball and the almost magical way it seemed to keep finding the flag.

Each time he sets himself before a shot, Greg Norman's body has a kind of quiver that also triggers a leg movement as he grounds his feet, which also move. The most frequent twitch, however, is in his grip, which he sets and resets, checks and rechecks, several times before each shot. In fact, Greg is one of the slowest players on tour, just like his onetime idol Jack Nicklaus. He is so slow that the impatient, impetuous John Daly once hit into his group at another tournament. That had made Greg and Tony very angry, and Tony had spoken to Daly, warning him not to do such a thing again.

Greg didn't speak to Daly, but he does sometimes talk during a round of golf. Playing the second round of the 1993 Tour Championship with Nick Price, Greg chatted with Nick occasionally as they made their way around the Olympic Club's Lake Course. But the conversation was still minimal. On the short uphill par-four seventh, where Nick sank a beautiful lag putt, all Greg said was, "Nice putt, Nick."

"Thank you," was Nick's equally laconic reply.

On the next hole, also uphill, a par three, Price hit out of the bunker located above the hole and his ball stopped about four feet from the cup. This was the hole that Greg would ace at the same tournament the following year. Nick's nice bunker shot elicited no comment from Greg, who had a chip to contend with. But later in the round, when Price chipped in on the seventeenth for an incredible par, Greg smiled, slapped Price's back, and said, "Nice par, Nick."

This was as loquacious as he usually ever becomes during a tournament.

Now, silently approaching the eighteenth green at Hartford, a serene Norman aimed a seven-iron right at the flag, and his ball hit the pin before stopping four feet from the hole for an easy birdie putt. Norman was eight under, and he still had his back nine—the course's front—to come.

Though he continued to hit the ball well, the putts stopped dropping, and when he reached the tee of his last hole he was nine under. Trying to cut off too much of the corner of a dogleg right, he pushed his drive, this time into deep fescue. Before a marshal had reached the place, a girl picked up the ball, thinking it was a souvenir.

"Hey!" an older man shouted. "That's the Shark's ball!"

Frightened, the girl dropped it and ran. When Norman arrived at the spot, someone told him what had happened and he called for an official to give him a ruling.

In the 1993 Fred Meyer Challenge, Chi Chi Rodriguez's drive at the second hole at the Oregon Golf Club landed in the long grass before reaching the fairway. After searching for the ball, he managed to hit it out with what looked like a sand wedge, then took his driver and almost put the ball on the green, from where he nearly chipped in for what would have been a miracle par. Though I had never seen a pro hit this poor a tee shot, I had often seen pros, after they had been in trouble on the course, move quickly and forcefully to put their misfortune behind them. One of the most distinguishing features of a pro's game is this ability to get out of trouble—an ability that is obviously founded in large part on technical skill, but which also manifests itself as an extremely determined demonstration of will.

Announcers on television and fans at golf tournament frequently say, "They make it look easy," but there was nothing easy about the shot that faced Greg Norman on this last hole at the GHO. The shot was so hard as to look virtually impossible.

Even before the official arrived to give Greg his ruling, the Shark had noticed the refreshment stand ahead that stood as an obstruction between him and the green. For some reason, this stand had been placed in bounds.

After listening to the man who had seen the ball picked up, the official let Greg drop his ball at that spot. After the drop, his line to the green was now obstructed, so he was allowed to find a place no nearer the hole where there was no such obstruction and drop again. His ball still lay in deep fescue, but it was sitting up nicely. The Shark hit a hard wedge and the ball traveled all the way to the green, where he two-putted.

Reflecting later on the round, Greg admitted that he had "played great. Seventeen good holes. I played as good as I have any day since Memorial or Kemper."

FLASH BACKWARDS: The shark has just won the 1995 Memorial. Now his face and figure fill a full-page ad for King Cobra golf clubs, placed strategically in the middle of *Golf World*'s editorial coverage of the tournament. Holding his King Cobra metal driver—9 degrees loft, deep face, True Temper Dynamic Gold steel shaft, X-400 flex, 43 1/2 inches long, Golf Pride Tour Wrap Cord grip (size 58), swingweight D-3—Greg appears to be watching in flight the Maxfli HT balata 100 compression ball (with SHARK printed on it, on the other side of the ball from the number 0, the number that is always printed on his golf balls) that he has just hit, no doubt for another of the birdies that propelled him to a final score of nineteen under. His mouth is slightly open, revealing a few of his perfect teeth (which he had capped with the winnings from his first pro tournament). But his lips are slightly pursed, with the hint of a frown rather than his characteristic smile, and his eyes appear to be squinting somewhat. There is a slight tilt to the torso. A little of the blond hair shows below the black straw hat and behind the neck.

Handsome fellow.

"We make believers," the copy proclaims. There is no need to add an exclamation mark.

But there is apparently always a need to reinforce the message of such ads. In the Shark's world, the line between hype and fact is often blurred. For a short time after he started Great White Shark Enterprises, Greg employed a man who was formerly director of information for the PGA Tour, Tom Place. One of Place's duties was to put out press releases about the Shark. A three-page handout at the 1994 Masters was headed, simply, "Greg Norman," and began with Greg's "1994 World-wide Performances." The Shark's career Masters record followed, with a "Career Victories" summary on page two listed year by year and summarized in two special categories, "Victories by Country" (Australia 28 down to Wales 1) and "Victories by Territory." Another press release, dated a few weeks before the Masters, presented canned quotes under the rubric "Greg Norman . . . His Thoughts About the Augusta National Golf Club and the Masters Tournament." No other competitor had such publicity, or the panache to put it out. But the power of the Shark's image was so great that the release seemed in keeping with his persona. There was even a certain poignancy to the text's introduction, which noted that though Greg "still is seeking his first Green Jacket, he has been ever so close on several occasions."

Ever so close. In 1986, the year before he lost to 1987 Masters champion Larry Mize in a playoff when Mize chipped in on the eleventh hole (the second playoff hole), Norman would have been in a playoff against Jack Nicklaus had he not bogeyed the eighteenth. His final-round score in 1986 was 70, five shots higher than Jack's. His final-round score in 1987 was 72, a critical shot poorer than Mize. The next year, 1988, he had a terrific 64 in the finale, but that was only good for fifth place, coming as it did in a tournament that he started with a 77. Ever so far.

HE WAS A wounded Shark when he lost to the man who was now his new neighbor, Nick Price, in the inaugural event of Shell's Wonderful World of Golf (actually an old series revived, with two top players pitted against each other in stroke play). Ahead in the match, which was contested at his own course, the Medalist, located down the street from his Hobe Sound estate, Norman made some mistakes on the back nine and lost to Price by four strokes.

"Oh, Greg, don't pull it," he said on the twelfth tee, a long par three. "You dummy. You dummy."

In the spring of 1995, at Doral, in a tournament he had won two years before, Norman pulled his drive slightly left on the eighteenth hole and had a difficult lie. Needing a four to win and a five to tie Nick Faldo for a playoff, Norman went for the green, protected by water, and badly pulled his approach, triggering the familiar sound of a splash, which would in turn be followed by the familiar cries of his critics. The carping intensified later at the Kemper Open, when Norman was in the hunt only to push his tee shot right at the par-three seventeenth for another splash.

"Oh dear," said CBS announcer Ben Wright on national TV.

Furious with Wright when he learned of the criticism, Norman told the announcer he had defended him during a recent controversy regarding remarks Wright was alleged by a reporter to have made about lesbianism and the women's professional golf tour. The Shark wouldn't be sticking up for Ben anymore.

And Greg was even angrier at the editor of *Golf Digest*, Jerry Tarde, who wrote in a column: "He's gone further on less performance than any athlete in the world. And he's done it by leaving Australia and coming to the United States, living here, raising his family here, running his businesses here, enjoying all the freedoms and opportunities of America, getting rich beyond imagination on American dollars. Norman is the Madonna of golf. He's the natural by-product of a world run by marketing types who believe perception always exceeds reality."

The two men got together for lunch at Hartford, where Norman gave Tarde a piece of his mind: "You've written the article," Greg said. "People have drawn conclusions. It hurt my family and my name. You're wrong. Your facts are wrong. You prejudiced me and a lot of it wasn't correct."

Standing by what he wrote, which he said was directed against "Greg Norman the corporate icon," Tarde agreed to write a letter of apology to Norman's wife for hurting her feelings. But, he said afterward, he could not believe Greg had threatened to leave the PGA Tour because of something that anyone had written. "It's way out of proportion."

Everything about Greg Norman was out of proportion. The specific event that raised Tarde's ire—the announcement prior to the 1994 Shark Shootout of a World Tour—was out of proportion, or would have been had it involved any other golfer but Greg. The World Tour proposal, in which thirty top players were to compete against one another in tournaments televised on Rupert Murdoch's global television empire, was stonewalled by tour commissioner Deane Beman's successor, Tim Finchem. Anyone participating, Finchem announced, would risk expulsion from the regular tour.

Not one pro, not even Nick Price, signed up to participate in the World Tour, and the idea was quickly dropped. By March, when Greg began his season at Doral (his only other 1995 appearance on the American tour having been the early-January Mercedes Championships), he was almost contrite, going out of his way to greet fellow players and trying to act like one of the guys.

But Greg Norman would never be able to be one of the guys. His image had seen to that. Around the time of the World Tour announcement he went on two advertising shoots conducted by the Boston firm Hill, Holliday to film sequences for a new Sharkwear campaign that would debut in 1995. "Attack life" was the theme of the campaign, which by the time the United States Open was contested at Shinnecock Hills on Long Island in June would be launched in New York with a huge billboard likeness of Greg and similar shots on New York subways. The phenomenal commercial success of this campaign combined with Norman's own superb play on the golf course—he won twice on tour in June, and arguably could have won four times, with a record month of $781,780 in official earnings.

With a somewhat stagnating market in golf, Sharkwear has

been repositioning itself to capture the casual market. Shark-wear was selling $200 million of clothing and accessories by late 1994.

For a Sharkwear shoot last winter at the Black Diamond Ranch in Florida, Norman kept Hill, Holliday staff and an expensive photographer waiting several hours because fog had grounded his helicopter. He finally had to fly to the shoot in his Gulfstream. Then he drove himself in a golf cart to the area of the ranch where the crew was waiting. At least one of those people, account representative Meredith Maren, will never forget her first sight of the Shark as he made his entrance.

"Suddenly, over a knoll, there he was, wearing a yellow sweater and with that blond hair. What an amazing aura he had about him." And Maren remembers "the intensity of his eyes, how he walked, how he carried himself. He has an amazing confidence."

But it was a challenging shoot. At one point, art director Simon Bowden was afraid that an impatient Shark was going to leave the shoot because of the necessity of retakes.

"Someone suggested I tell him one of my off-color jokes," Maren remembers. "That worked. We bonded."

Now, in two days, after he went on to win the GHO, the Shark would not only claim his fourteenth tour victory but vault himself into the top place on the year's money list and second on the all-time money list.

"I'm glad I can entertain people," he said. "But I can't wait for the day when I can go back to Australia with no commitments."

Inevitably, there were questions about the weekend at Shinnecock, when he had made only one birdie over the last two rounds. What had happened?

It was an old question.

Maybe he had looked at tapes of the Open? Perhaps Saturday's disappointing round?

"No. I didn't watch Saturday's round. My wife taped all the rounds. I don't usually watch, even when I win. Could I have shot eighty-five? Yes. But I could have shot seventy."

A score of 70 that day would have won the tournament for him, but he had no regrets, he insisted. The important thing, he stressed, was how often he kept putting himself in a position to win. He had a saying for that, as it seemed he did for anything he was asked: "Unless you're out there beating the drum, you never hear the tune."

HE HAD BEEN beating the drum coming into the 1995 U.S. Open at Shinnecock, the same course where in 1986 he had lost not only the fourth-round lead but his composure as well. A heckler had bothered him that day, and he had finally challenged the man to meet him afterward. They hadn't met, but the Shark lost to Raymond Floyd.

He said, now, he had put the incident behind him, just as he said he had put the loss to Floyd behind him, the other major championship losses, all the well-known, well-documented disappointments of his career. Stating this had become a kind of mantra for Norman, but the act of speaking this way was not something he had put behind him. He repeated its basic form every time he was asked a question about his past. Someday, one hoped, Norman would simply learn to say, "Next question."

Two days before the 1995 tournament got underway, the Shark said he had only "faint memories" of 1986.

"I don't have distinct memories of how the golf course played," he continued. But, he added, he had heard the course setup for the 1995 event was excellent.

Competing at Shinnecock after a win at Memorial and a fourth at the Kemper, Norman exuded even more confidence than usual, if that was possible. His terrific golf in June had surprised some people, because he had been out six weeks since a bad back had forced him to withdraw from the Heritage in

April. He had actually teed it up in that tournament and withdrawn after his first drive, which meant he was immediately disqualified from winning the Vardon Trophy, given by the PGA of America to the tour player with the lowest stroke average. This was an award that meant a lot to Norman. He had been very angry in 1993 when he learned he had not played the requisite number of rounds to win that year's Vardon. Nick Price won it instead. This past April, with a chance to beat his pal in 1995, and anyone else that wanted to give him a run, Norman was irate over the news that under the PGA rules the Heritage withdrawal would disqualify him for consideration. Petulantly, he even threatened to boycott the PGA Championship in August, the last major championship of the year and the only one conducted by the PGA of America (a separate organization from the PGA Tour).

By the time he had flown to Long Island for the Open, Greg had calmed down. He was his usual straight-ahead self again. Before returning to the tour he had taken a week to recuperate and then five weeks to fish and dive and work out. "Downtime" he called this. He spent as much of it as he could with his family, whom he referred to his as "best friends." He had to work at avoiding the public during his downtime; when he was out on his boat, he said, he didn't even go to the marina. He liked to stay on the boat for a week to ten days without a break. He had taken those five weeks in the spring every year since 1988, when he moved to south Florida.

"Being mentally and physically fit gave me the enthusiasm, the desire, to get back out there and play very fresh," he confessed. He was proud of this fitness, which he ascribed in part to his study of such books as *Zen and the Martial Arts*, a slim volume by Hollywood screenwriter Joe Hyams. In a reverse turn of phrase, Norman said that one of the things he had learned from such study was that the "mind follows the body," by which he meant that if you have a fit body your mind will be sharper.

He was fit a week before the Memorial. "When I knew I was playing the Friday before, I went home, saw my wife, said to her, 'I am ready to go. I wish the tournament was starting this weekend.'"

Norman was completely unapologetic for how the Kemper had ended. The seventeenth—the par three he double-bogeyed when his fourth-round tee shot went in the water—"was a product of the fifteenth hole," he explained.

"When I hit the putt on fifteen, I thought I made it, and it just dived across the front of the hole. At that stage, I was eleven under. The leaders, they were thirteen under. So when I got to seventeen, I was two back with two to go. Under normal circumstances, I probably wouldn't have gone directly at the pin. The wind was blowing off the right. I aimed halfway between the pin and the water. I just pushed it ten feet. That is all it was."

Next question.

Now he was at the Open. "I really don't foresee things just falling apart and disappearing," he blurted out. "It is just a matter of going along and doing what I have been doing last week at Kemper or the week before at Memorial."

Or was it?

In his great, persistent certainty that everything was okay, Greg sometimes sounded a hollow note. Positive thinking might lead to positive results, but why couldn't the Shark ever confess he was scared?

"I feel like I have gone a little higher up the ladder, playability-wise," he said on the eve of the Open, referring to his growth as a golfer from his twenties and thirties to the age of forty. "I am not as wildly aggressive as I used to be in my twenties," he continued. "And in my thirties I was aggressive. Now I am more controlled aggression. I think that is a good way of putting it. I have control, the best word in the book, even though I think my game, swingwise, is better than what it was in my twenties and thirties.

"I think my putting is about the same. It is a little more consistent than it was in the past. I am not a twenty-one- or twenty-four-putts-a-round guy, because I feel like I hit a lot of greens. If you miss a lot of greens, that is when you get it down to twenty-one. I'd like to have twenty-four putts and hit eighteen greens. That is a beautiful score."

It was beautiful talk. The Shark was in super form, speech-wise. Would his form hold up, golfwise?

WHO CAN EXPLAIN what happens to a golfer's emotions when he realizes during a major championship that he has a chance to win?

It is a question many golfers are never in a position to answer. For some, just getting into the United States Open or one of the other majors is achievement enough. For others, anything short of victory is failure.

For better or worse, Greg Norman is one of the latter. It is a role he has given himself.

There are people in the golf world who think that the Shark puts too much pressure on himself to win, especially in major championships. What did the Shark feel at Shinnecock, where he was now the favorite?

"I'd rather have that than being a forgotten horse somewhere in the back there," he said. "I always put that type of pressure on myself anyway. Whenever I play in a golf tournament I go out there with the intention of winning the golf tournament. To me, finishing second, third, or fifth—or twentieth—doesn't make much difference to me."

It was a credo that sold a lot of Sharkwear. But, so far, it had won Greg Norman exactly zero U.S. Open titles, which was also the total of his Masters victories and PGA Championships.

ON A SUNNY, windy Thursday afternoon, Greg Norman stood at the first tee, looking for all the world as if he'd won this tournament every year he'd played in it. His threesome the first two days of the tournament would include Paul Azinger, back on tour after his successful bout with cancer, and Raymond Floyd, the man who had beaten the Shark here in 1986. Azinger, who had resumed playing competitively late the previous summer, had still not found the form that had made him one of the top professionals in the late 1980s and early 1990s. Floyd, whose '86 Shinnecock victory had been very emotional, now played most of his golf on the Senior Tour, where he had met great success.

For the first four holes at Shinnecock, Norman played fine golf, hitting the ball solidly and just missing putts on two and four that would have given him an early score of two under par. Instead, as he teed off on the fifth hole—the only par five on the front nine—he still stood at par.

At 535 yards long, the fifth is easily reachable in two strokes for a pro of Norman's strength. With the wind with him, even a good amateur might be able to get home in two, perhaps hitting a three-wood for his second shot. But the landing area for a golfer's drive is relatively narrow, with much bunkering and very punishing rough to hinder anyone missing the fairway. And the green itself had become firmer in the afternoon wind and sun, so that only an fine approach would hold.

Norman hit a perfect drive, right into the throat of the fairway. In three days, with the tournament on the line, he would have the breeze to his back and go for this green with a seven-iron, his ball landing on the green and bouncing past to set up a chip and two putts for a costly par. But today, with the wind in his face, Greg needed much more than a seven-iron. He chose a three-wood.

The ball took off on a high trajectory and came to rest just short of the green. On his next shot Norman nearly chipped in for eagle; his short putt for birdie left him one under, with the long par-four sixth ahead. Now, however, he would have the wind behind him.

A tremendous drive almost reached the pond guarding the green from the right side. Greg studied the sucker pin, perched tantalizingly above a large bunker below the left portion of the elevated green. The prudent shot was to land his ball on the right and take two putts for the par.

Eschewing caution, Greg aimed directly at the flag.

The shot was perfect, the kind of first-round shot that, if followed with a birdie putt, can be recalled in the glow of victory on Sunday as crucial.

Greg missed the putt.

It was no time to feel sorry for himself. Invariably, anyone who does that in golf soon has greater problems.

One of the things he had learned from his reading was an almost rhythmic alternation of focus and withdrawal. The term "full pressure" stood for focus; for withdrawal, Greg thought of the word "relax."

Full pressure.

Relax.

Full pressure.

Relax.

In a golf round, full pressure was of course the moment just before and during each shot. Then, before the next shot, there was an opportunity to relax—not in the sense of taking a break, but of withdrawing momentarily from the incredibly intense concentration and effort that was required to hit a world-class shot in the world-class tension of the United States Open.

Full pressure: the putt for par on the sixth.

Relax: the walk to the seventh tee.

Full pressure: the long-iron tee shot on seven, a par three of 188 yards, modeled on the so-called Redan Hole of the famed North Berwick course.

And what a shot it was! Right at the flag, landing and rolling left, but remaining pin-high on this treacherously tilted green.

By now the word was getting around the golf grapevine at the course that Greg was playing especially well. The number of people following him and his group, already in the thousands, grew.

Greg walked to the seventh green and marked his ball. A birdie would move him to two under.

He scored a par.

On eight, his tee shot landed in a bunker on the right side. Tony told him he had 125 yards to the front of the green. He caught the ball cleanly coming out of the trap, but it landed in some greenside rough. He was looking at his first bogey of the day.

He made a very poor pitch. Certain bogey now.

No! The long putt dropped for a four.

A fine drive, an approach to about twelve feet, and two putts gave him another par on nine. He had finished the front in one under. Those holes had taken two and a half hours to play.

On number ten, a difficult par four where a golfer's drive has little margin for error at the crest of a hill, followed by an approach over a valley, Greg pulled his second shot, but it landed on the green about twenty feet from the pin. He two-putted for another par.

In every round of golf, there is at least one sequence on which everything in that round seems to turn. The next three holes proved to be such a sequence for the Shark.

On number eleven, a short par three, his tee shot was short, ending in a bunker, and then he was strong coming out. Greg faced a very testing six-footer to save par.

He made the putt.

On the very long par-four twelfth, he drove into the right rough and then tried to get to the green instead of conceding a stroke to extricate himself from that rough. The five-iron approach landed in more rough, and the chip from there left him with another nail-biting six-footer.

He made the putt.

Greg took his stance on the elevated thirteenth tee and was about to begin his backswing when playing partner Raymond Floyd's voice startled him and everyone within earshot.

"Greg!" Floyd said loudly. "Wait a minute. There's a guy taking pictures."

A man in the gallery was snapping photographs, which was against tournament rules. It was also exceedingly distracting to the players. What would be the impact on Greg of this interruption in his concentration?

He killed his drive. He nailed his approach. He made a five-footer for birdie to go two under.

That was still his score, an hour later, when the round ended. He had hit only nine fairways and twelve greens in regulation, but he had shot 68.

A car driven by a USGA official waited for him at the back entrance of the media tent, so he could make a quick escape after the obligatory press conference. ("It's a U.S. Open and you have to understand you're not going to hit every green and fairway. . . . I hit some crisp iron shots and hit the ball the right direction . . . saved some good pars, missed some makeable birdies. . . . It was give and take.")

At seven-thirty in the evening, a small group of fans watched him putting under the watchful eye of his coach, Butch Harmon. Harmon was disappointed that some of Greg's putts, particularly on the front nine, had not fallen. But that was golf. Switching from putting to chipping, Greg practiced a few more minutes. Then he pulled out his wallet and Rolex watch from a pocket in his golf bag and, surrounded by people begging for autographs, walked the short distance from the practice green to the clubhouse, where his wife met him.

Tony waited in the Chevy Tahoe that was pulled up in front of the clubhouse. He was as upbeat as his boss.

"Greg played great," Tony said.

It was early in the tournament, but maybe this was Greg's year. When he went to two under for the second round and four under for the tournament, after only three holes on Friday, and then hit a perfect drive on four, the number of photographers walking the ropes with the Shark's threesome grew, a sure sign that something *important* was happening. Even after the Shark cooled down for a long stretch—before chipping in with a sand wedge from the collar on eighteen!—there was a palpable sense among the men and women at Shinnecock that Greg was going to stay on his game. The wind would be picking up later in the day, which was certain to hinder the afternoon threesomes. Greg was sure to go out in the last group on Saturday. Why, if the wind kept blowing, all he would have to do was shoot par and he would probably remain in control of the tournament.

It was hard to disagree, even given the string of strange endings that read like a résumé in the Shark's career.

"Greg's going to win," predicted a veteran golf producer with ESPN on Friday night. That would certainly help weekend television ratings on NBC.

But, as Greg Norman knew perhaps better than anyone who had ever played professional golf, tournaments, especially major tournaments, don't finish on Friday.

SHARKBITE

THERE'S NO BETTER feeling in the world than when your caddie gives you yardage of one hundred eighty-five and a half yards, to be able to hit that ball within a foot and a half of where you want to hit it. That's what the pinnacle is all about. You don't get that all the time, but when you get it, there's nobody else in the world who can experience what you're experiencing. You have control over yourself. You have control over your mind. If you don't have control over your mind, then you don't have control over yourself.

Golf is such a complex makeup of an equation. It's difficult to gel those four or five things together in that equation to get the right answer. But I believe you do have control over it.

I focus on a shot—like the three-wood on number one at Olympic with out-of-bounds behind the hole, I aimed it right. There was a dead tree behind the green and the tree was just smack in the middle of the green. I aimed at the right-hand edge of a dead branch. I didn't aim at the tree, I aimed at a point on the branch of a tree. I could see a little knot on the branch and focused on that.

In a round of seventy let's say you take thirty putts, you take forty hits. So, in those forty hits, if I actually hit three or four shots perfect the way I wanted to hit them, that would be an exceptionally good day.

It's a wonderful sense of satisfaction.

SUMMER 1995

"HOW'S YOUR GAME?" I asked Jack in the clubhouse.

"Terrible," answered Jack. "Can't hit a thing."

"What's the problem?" I inquired.

"I wish I knew."

"Yeah, I know what you mean. I've been having trouble the last month."

"I've had this problem for three years," said Jack.

Alistair was trying a new driver. His home course was closed for a tournament he wasn't in, so he'd come over this evening with the new driver and a few other clubs that he threw into a light bag. The new driver had a large head and a very long shaft, even longer than the super long shafts that some guys had been using the last year.

Alistair took the driver out of his bag. Then he let the bag drop on the ground and walked to the first tee, where he took a few practice swings. He made a big turn in his backswing, something he'd been working on, and he came off the ball on his backswing, like Curtis Strange. But he didn't drive the ball the distance Strange did. Alistair probably drove the ball 230 or 240 yards. That was about twenty to thirty yards below the average you needed to play consistently good golf on difficult courses. Of course you also had to be able to hit good iron shots, chip the ball, and putt. Probably, thought Alistair, hitting good iron shoots was the single most distinguishing feature of a pro's game. The distances a pro got with his irons, the crisp contact, the bull's-eye accuracy: that was very impressive. Awesome really. But first you had to get the ball in the fairway.

Alistair stood at the first tee and practiced doing just that.

"I'm going to land the ball by the one-fifty marker," he said, referring to the white disk in the middle of the fairway, two hundred and forty yards from the tee. The disk was called the one-fifty marker because it measured one hundred and fifty yards from the center of the green.

Alistair's first drive landed in the rough, to the left of his target.

He teed up another ball and choked up slightly on the club.

This shot landed in the fairway, right where he had said it would.

"I'm playing in the Open next week and it's a course that really suits my game," he said. He meant the Massachusetts Open, not the U.S. Open. The course was in Concord, Massachusetts, an old course with lots of trees and small greens. A shot maker's course.

Alistair was a shotmaker.

But first you had to drive the ball in the fairway.

It was hot, and Alistair was sweating.

"Hate this hot weather," he said. He was from Scotland and he'd never become used to hot, humid days. He played golf every day he could, except when it was too hot. Then he hit balls early in the morning or late, like this, when the sun was setting and it was soon so dark he wouldn't be able to see the flight of his ball.

"Let me hit one more," he said on the first. He didn't choke up this time. The ball took off straight at the one-fifty marker and almost hit the marker on one bounce.

"That's the way I need to play in Concord," Alistair said.

Alas, he didn't, but his disappointment was short-lived. In a qualifying tournament for the United States Amateur, he finished in a tie for the last spot that qualified. On the first play-off hole, he was the only competitor to put his drive in the fairway. "I just happened to hit the best drive I've ever hit," he said later. His subsequent par was good enough to win the playoff. Elated, he walked back to the clubhouse, "but I couldn't feel my feet touch the grass," he said. On his way home that evening, he called his wife to share the amazing news.

"I don't know if this is really true," he said to her. "I've got this piece of paper in my hand that says I qualified for the Amateur."

It was difficult to imagine Corey Pavin's being any happier when he hit a four-wood from the fairway on the eighteenth hole to clinch victory in the 1995 United States Open. Or Ben Crenshaw, after his emotional 1995 Masters win that came as a coda to the death of his longtime teacher, Harvey Pennick. Or John Daly, who won his second major with the 1995 British Open, and Australian Steve Elkington, who captured his first with the 1995 PGA Championship. What separates such golfers as Alistair from the professionals is a degree of physical and mental skill that is discernible and palpable. But they all play the same game.

"If I could tie fishline with hooks at both ends from my mouth to my dick, maybe I could learn to keep my head down."

Another of my golfing companions was talking. We were standing on the ninth tee, and this man had been slicing the ball badly all day. He knew what the problem was. But he didn't seem to know how to cure it, though his brother is a club pro in Florida.

"Corey Pavin, he sure had kept his head down at the Open. On that four-wood. Smoked it."

"What a shot," another of the foursome said. "That was it for Greg on that one."

I thought of a remark about Greg that I had heard on television. "Greg Norman has so many seconds they'll bury him in a silver coffin," said *Sports Illustrated*'s Rick Reilly before the last round of the Open at Shinnecock.

Then the Shark went out in the last group, tied for the lead, and hit a great drive and a fine iron into the first green and missed the birdie putt. On the second he hit another fine iron but he pulled it ever so slightly and had to chip onto the green. His par putt of four or five feet was short. Bogey. End of lead.

He missed the third green with his approach but made a great chip and saved par. On four he hit the green in two but missed the birdie putt. He had by then gone 22 consecutive holes without a birdie, the last birdie having come on the eighteenth hole in Friday's second round. Now he faced the par-five fifth, a must-birdie hole. He reached it in two with a driver and a *seven-iron*.

He should have hit an eight.

The ball bounced just in front of the green and rolled all the way across its slick surface, leaving him with a very hard chip and two putts for par.

"Greg Norman is the best looking puncher, the best looking fighter out here," said former Open winner and current NBC announcer Johnny Miller.

But if he was, why the wrong shot at five? It was reminiscent of the seventeenth hole at the 1995 Masters, when he had pulled his wedge and effectively lost the tournament.

Why?

It is the kind of question a magazine writer posed in print after the Shark's 1995 Memorial victory. Greg didn't speak to the man for three months.

Attack life.

Later in the summer, after the majors were over, he did win another tournament, the World Series of Golf, and he won it amidst controversy. During the first round, he accused playing partner Mark McCumber of cheating—he said McCumber had touched the line of his putt when McCumber said he was swatting away an insect. Refusing to sign McCumber's scorecard afterwards, the Shark was going to withdraw from the tournament, he was so angry. But his wife and new commissioner Tim Finchem convinced him to play. He won in a playoff with a chip-in, the kind of shot it seemed other people were always making to beat him.

The victory, his third of an extraordinary campaign, secured Greg's place atop the year's money list, on which the indefatigable Patrick Burke finished a remarkable 115th and the rebounding Scott Verplank an inspiring 55th. The Shark was now the all-time leading money winner in PGA Tour history, with over nine million dollars. His dominance of the Sony rankings also increased. With a win late in the fall at the Australian Open, he widened his Sony lead over second-place golfer Nick Price (on a list that put Brad Faxon 30th). Nevertheless, as an Australian, he was ineligible to compete in the Ryder Cup competition held in Rochester, New York, in September, a biennial competition between teams from America and Europe.

With a record 63 in the final round of the PGA Championship, Brad Faxon had qualified for the American team. At one point in the round it appeared he might break 60, something only two golfers had ever done in an American professional tournament, and a feat never achieved in a major. Eventually Brad needed to make a long putt on the eighteenth to secure the 63, a score that held up for fifth place and just enough Ryder Cup points to earn him a coveted spot on the team.

The week before the three-day contest, he played again in the B.C. Open, despite the fact that his wife Bonnie had just given birth to the couple's third child, another daughter, whom they named Sophie.

I drove to Rochester to watch some of the tournament, which began on a day of deluge. The golf went on, of course, wet as it was. Playing in a four-ball afternoon match with Peter Jacobsen as his partner, Brad Faxon hit his drive into the water on the seventh hole and had to take a drop from the hazard at a penalty of one stroke. Jacobsen mistook Faxon's final stroke on the hole for a par putt—somehow, Jacobsen had missed seeing the penalty drop—and, because only the better of each player's scores counted on each hole, Jacobsen then chipped strong from off the green for birdie. When the ball didn't go in the hole he picked it up.

"Nice par," he said to Brad, who then had to correct the astonished Jacobsen. Under the rules of the competition, Jacobsen could not now replace his ball and putt for par. The team's score for the hole went down as bogey five, and they went on to lose the match.

On Saturday, the skies had cleared and it was sunny and brisk at Oak Hill, an old design by the famed Scot, Donald Ross, that had been the site of many championships over the years. Across Monroe Road from the back side of the course, Pittsford Plaza was crowded with cars and buses, but Rochester life went on. This was a tough ticket, because sales had been limited, but you could have driven by Pittsford Plaza and mistaken the hubbub for a high school football rally.

More than 300 years ago, where devoted fans now strained for a glimpse of the golfers coming up the fourteenth fairway, an army of 3,000 Frenchmen and Indians crossed these grounds on their way to battle under a general named Denonville. What this had to do with golf was anyone's guess, but it was duly noted on a historical marker. In fact, Oak Hill seemed filled with plaques. Nearby, above the thirteenth green, each tree in a stand of oaks had been dedicated with a plaque memorializing well-known golfers, most of whom had done something special at Oak Hill. In 1968, Lee Trevino won the U.S. Open here, in a victory that effectively began his career as a dominant player. In prose that was extraordinary for its condescension, the plaque on Lee's oak referred indirectly to his

Mexican-American background (not the usual ancestry for membership at Oak Hill). It read, "Inspiration to those of humble beginning."

Walking behind one of the matches, I ran into a writer friend who told me he was going up in an F-14 with Greg Norman in December. The original date had been the week following the Ryder Cup, but then Greg learned he had to play in one more American tournament to have the requisite number of rounds to become Player of the Year (he already had enough points to win).

Later, I bumped into Brad Faxon's father, who confessed he had been too nervous to eat lunch. He was following his son's afternoon match closely, making comments shot by shot. When Brad's drive on the eighth hole went right, toward some trees, his father shook his head, "He had lots of practice on that shot, especially when he was starting out." Before the next shot he said, "Come on, Brad. Hit it straight."

And his son did, through much of the rest of the day and well into the finale on Sunday, until he came to the last hole, needing a par to tie his match with David Gilford. Both men drove well, but Gilford skied a four wood beyond the green and into the deep fringe, leaving the proverbial door open to Faxon. By this time in the tournament, the lead the United States had been protecting since Friday had vanished, and the pressure on the golfers was extraordinary. Faxon hit his approach into a bunker in front of the green, but when Gilford left his chip in the tall grass and hit the following chip—his fourth stroke on the hole—Brad definitely had the advantage. Even after his bunker shot came out a little strong and ran ten feet past the hole, it still seemed the hole was his.

Gilford made his putt.

Later, after tears during a television interview, after Curtis Strange had missed his own change at par on this hole (and the two previous ones), after the U.S. had in fact *lost the Cup,* Brad said, "If I had one thing to do over, I would have taken longer to read the putt."

It had missed the hole to the right.

"I was so sure I was going to make it as I stood over it," Faxon said later. "I was actually thinking about what it was going to feel like when it went in. I couldn't believe it when I missed."

After skipping the Disney tournament in Orlando, Brad again hit the road, hoping to earn enough money in the last two tournaments of the season to qualify for the Tour Championship. He fell short, finishing the season in 37th place.

That same weekend, the Shark was in England to play for Australia in an event called the Dunhill Cup. There, in a first-round match, he lost to a relatively unknown Argentinian named Jose Coceres. Despite victories on Saturday and Sunday, his team was eliminated. Greg flew home to begin preparations for the Tour Championship, held this year in Oklahoma. Would things work out differently for him than they had in San Francisco?

I watched that tournament on television, which is also where I had watched part of the Ryder Cup when I was at Oak Hill. The driving range for the Ryder Cup players was actually part of a second Oak Hill course, otherwise closed during Cup week. I wandered over there on Saturday afternoon, where Philip Walton, a Ryder Cup rookie on the European team, was the lone golfer practicing at the time. That morning, with his partner Ian Woosnam, he had lost a foursomes match to the American team of Loren Roberts and Peter Jacobsen. The match had gone to the last hole.

The next day, Walton would win the climactic singles match against Jay Haas, watched by millions of people around the world. But on this Saturday afternoon on the range, he practiced by himself, while the few dozen fans in the area stared at a huge projection-screen television picture that loomed over the area. I took a seat with them and watched Brad Faxon make a putt in the same match that, earlier, I had watched in person with his father.

It was 3:15 P.M. Despite the cool breeze, one man was asleep on the ground without his shirt, as if he were at the beach. At the far end of the range a helicopter, with a golfing or business dignitary on board, was preparing to take off. Soon, the loud roar of its engine drowned out the rustle of oak leaves nearby. Then, its propeller whirring, the helicopter left the ground.

With his caddy following, Walton walked from the range's hitting area to a bunker, where he practiced his sand shots. Six Ryder Cup marshalls wearing matching black pants and maroon jackets appeared to retrieve the balls that Sunday's unlikely hero had just hit on the range. I glanced at the television screen one more time, and then I left the range, too. I was eager to watch a little more golf. You never knew what you were going to find.

ACKNOWLEDGMENTS

MY EXTENDED FOURSOME is a fairly large one, and I owe thanks to many people for their help and encouragement throughout this project.

PGA Tour officials were friendly and cooperative. Special thanks to Denise Taylor, Sid Wilson, John Morris, Steve Rankin, Dave Lancer, Marty Caffey, Wes Seeley, Leslie Sinadinos, and Dianne Reed.

Among the people who helped me at tour events, thanks to Alex Alexander, Barbara Brewer, Geri Glaser, Scott Fenton, Bill and Jeri Johnson, Carol Kellogg, Ted Mingolla, Cathy Scherzer, Stan Wood, and Cindy Zeller.

At the USGA, my thanks to Suzanne Colson, Andrew Mutch, Rich Skyzinski, and Craig Smith. At the PGA of America, thanks to Holly Brown.

Also on the road, my thanks to David Coker at Sea Pines, Ted Danforth, Myra Foster at Stratton, and the Valentines. Thanks to Chris Mathewson at Ray Cook Golf Company, Bob Cantin and Stuart Miller at Ping, Doug Robinson at Foot-Joy, Kathleen Miller at IMG, Toby Zwikel, and Frank Williams, Nina Toscano, and Lynne Cook at Great White Shark Enterprises. And thanks to Preferred Travel and the Travel Loft.

Thanks also to Jaime Diaz, Lily Lie, Rick Reilly, and Tim Rosaforte at *Sports Illustrated;* Larry Dorman at the *New York Times;* Ken Burger, John Feinstein, Chip McGrath, David Rosenbaum, Adam Rothberg, Herbert Warren Wind, and WM.

For typing and editorial help, thanks to Joe Bills, Happi Cramer, Stephen Lee, and Mike O'Brien. For manuscript suggestions, thanks to Bonnie and Alistair Catto, Lolis Eric Elie, Tracy Kidder, Boom Boom Madden, Tracy Mehr, David and Sheldon Monette, Stuart Schoffman, Kim Townsend, and Nils Vigeland. Thanks also to Jonathan Dee, Jay Demerath, Bill Fuller, Joe Hamill, Steve Lembke, Jim and Beth MacDonald, Harris Pastides, John Ritter, Ed and Dave Twohig, and Jack Wideman.

Helping to keep me on the road were Gwen Briere, Doc-oh! Burke, Tim Clegg, Norton and Rikki Grubb, Mary J. Hebert, William E. Hart, Stanley Lachtara, Jacques C. Nordeman, the John Raschella family, and Nat Reed.

My sojourn began with a luncheon conversation in New York with my editor, Hilary Hinzmann. Wearing his Shark cap, he saw me through many nineteenth hole conversations, often by phone, often on Friday afternoons. So did my agent, Denise Shannon at the Georges Borchardt agency, where DeAnna Heindel and others thoughtfully talked golf when I called. Thank you, all.

At home, Maren learned to putt and Anna and Bonnie came along for golf walks. Out on the course Al Sorenson and Hugh Clark listened to many of the stories in this book while winning countless Nassaus and presses from me. On the tour itself, I am grateful to all the golfers and others associated with the professional game for the time they gave me, but I especially wish to thank Brad Faxon and Greg Norman. My son, who read this book in manuscript and offered numerous suggestions, also plays golf. We'd like to challenge the Shark and Fax to a match, if they'd give us a stroke a hole.